T0308001

BÉATRICE COINTREAU

ORGANIC WINE

A MARKETER'S GUIDE

Wine Appreciation Guild
San Francisco

Organic Wine: A Marketer's Guide

Text copyright © 2015 Béatrice Cointreau

Wine Appreciation Guild

an imprint of

Board and Bench Publishing

www.boardandbench.com

Editor: Margaret Clark

Book design: TIPS Technical Publishing, Inc.

Cover design: Tressa Pack

Cataloging-in-Publication data on file with the Library of Congress

ISBN: 978-1-935879-63-3
ePDF: 978-1-935879-62-6
ePub: 978-1-935879-46-6

Printed and bound in the U.S.A.

Contents

Preface

When I arrived in California, I quickly realized that health food stores were very popular and depending on the day, there were farmers' markets on almost every corner, with organic food and wine.

In terms of the distinctions between the organic labels for food and wine in the United States, it can be confusing even for organic buyers like me. In both cases, "organic" products must contain 95 percent of organic ingredients, which takes into account technological additives for which there are no organic alternatives. However, in the organic food category, the "made with..." label means that the product must contain a minimum of 70 percent of organic ingredients. For example, a sauce made from organic tomatoes but with conventional onions cannot be an "organic sauce," but rather a sauce "made with organic tomatoes."

Given that wine is essentially a single ingredient product, wines that only mention that they are "made with organic grapes" are made entirely of organic grapes. So I asked myself: "What is the difference between a wine that is certified 'organic' and a wine 'made with organic grapes' in the United States?"

In terms of content, the answer is added sulfites (up to 100 parts per million, or $1/2000^{th}$ of an ounce per glass), and that's all. But in terms of the label, only the first can be stamped with the green USDA organic seal, which is easy to understand and helps producers appeal to customers looking for "green" products. Initially, I found it difficult to understand this distinction, which has both advantages and drawbacks.

It was even more surprising for me because the American regulations differ from the new European regulations which, beginning with the 2012 harvest, allow winemakers to use the "organic wine" label (previously, only the words "wine made with organic grapes" were allowed) since a European committee agreed on the standards relating to organic wine practices, including the authorized addition of certain sulfites.

Consequently, "organic wine" has been left on uneven footing in the three-year trade agreement signed February 15, 2013 which recognizes the American and European organic programs as equivalent. Most of the certified products either in the United States or in the European Union can be sold as organic in both places starting June 1, 2013, which removes the requirements for them to be certified a second time. American wines "made from organic grapes" may soon be sold as "organic" in Europe, but the European "organic" wines bottled with added sulfites must still sport the label "made with organic grapes" on the American markets. The same problem persists in the agreements between the United States and Canada, a country that has authorized sulfites in organic wine since 2009. This is a great improvement for the imports/exports of "organic wines," but because the regulations are different, it can still be very confusing.

Sulfur is a natural element authorized in organic winemaking as a non-toxic fungicide. Added during wine production or bottling, sulfur dioxide is a component that protects the wine from oxidation and microbes, keeping it fresh, stable and fault-free throughout non-refrigerated transport and storage. A small but growing number of producers make wines with no added sulfites. However, most winemakers believe that a small amount of sulfites is essential to ensure the high quality of wine destined for commercial distribution. For some wine specialists and experts, sulfites are even required to ensure aromatic length. On the other hand, the label must absolutely indicate "contains sulfites" to inform people who are sensitive to them (asthma, allergies, headaches, etc.).

The new European regulations concerning "organic wine" authorize a maximum of 100 parts per million for red wine (compared to 150 for conventional red wines) and 150 parts per million for white and rosé wines (compared to 200 for their conventional versions). Dessert wines can have an extra 30 parts per million because there is a typically higher need for sulfites to prevent the residual sugar from fermenting in the bottle. Canada authorizes up to 100 parts per million in its organic wines, whereas in the United States, there is a distinction between the levels authorized in "organic" wines and those in wines "made from organic grapes."

For now, let's save time and money. Instead of trying to change regulations, we should try to improve our knowledge of organic wine, labels and sulfites!

This is why this book has been written.

—Los Angeles, January 2015

Acknowledgments

Many thanks to:

Sandrine Cassidy Schmitt

Natacha Arnaud-Battandier

Nathalie Borges-Johnson

Chapter 1
Organics and the Paradox of Globalization

If you had to select between two 92-point wines of the same variety, appellation and price, but one was made with sustainable winegrowing practices and the other was not, would you choose the sustainable wine? What if it cost $5 more?

Research has been mixed on whether consumers are willing to pay more for eco-labeled wines, and yet the number of wineries adopting sustainable practices continues to rise. But a new study by a team of researchers in Italy, Spain and California claims winery owners believe sustainability makes economic sense in the long term.

The study, by researchers at Spain's Universitat de Barcelona, California's Sonoma State University and Italy's Università San Raffaele and Università degli Studi di Macerata, was presented this summer at the Academy of Wine Business Research Conference in Germany.

The authors note that more wineries are adopting sustainable, organic or biodynamic techniques in their vineyards. More than 1,800 grapegrowers and wineries have participated in the California Sustainable Winegrowing assessment, the first step toward receiving certification. Sonoma County Winegrowers has launched an effort to have every Sonoma winery certified sustainable by 2019. Multiple programs exist in other major wine nations.

Sustainability is generally defined as using business practices that are environmentally friendly, socially equitable in terms of treating employees and community fairly, and economically viable in the long term. In the wine industry, this means that sustainable-vineyard owners attempt to create healthy soil with compost and cover crops and by reducing the use of pesticides. They also try to avoid wasting water and energy in both vineyard and cellar. What's required varies by certification program.

It's not clear if consumers are interested in purchasing wines labeled as sustainable—or organic or biodynamic. A 2012 study by UCLA's Institute of the Environment and Sustainability showed that an eco-certification label had a mixed effect on consumers. "We found that respondents preferred eco-labeled wines over an otherwise identical counterpart, when the price was low and the wine was from a low-quality region," wrote the authors. "However, these preferences were reversed if the wine was expensive and from a high-quality region."[1]

For the new study, the international team of researchers surveyed 260 winery owners in Italy, Spain and California about whether they have adopted sustainable approaches, whether they have continued such practices and whether they see business benefits. The wineries were not asked whether they were certified.

Results show that a comparable percentage of wineries in all three countries saw a clear business benefit in implementing sustainability strategies. Only six percent indicated they had tried to implement sustainable practices and abandoned the effort.

The benefits the wineries saw varied by country. For example, many of the Spanish wineries believed they profited by highlighting their sustainable efforts to consumers, and improved their relationships with distributors. Being green or sustainable set them apart.

In Italy and California, however, winery owners found that adopting sustainable strategies actually allowed them to focus on cost reduction. They reported reducing waste and improving operational efficiencies. The authors noted at the conference that many surveyed wineries also believed that their wine tasted better, which was reason enough for them.

All of the wineries surveyed were small- or medium-size businesses, and many were family-owned, a fact linked to another common reason winery owners gave for going sustainable: They believe in preserving the environment—and their businesses—for future generations.

Spain's Miguel Torres said he began focusing on sustainability because of the threat of climate change.

"We did it because we live in the vineyard and we want our environment to be healthy for our family," said Peter Work, co-owner of Ampelos Cellars in California's Stanta Rita Hills. Ampelos is the first vineyard in the U.S. to become triple-certified in sustainable, organic and biodynamic practices. "Though it costs more money to farm this way, the benefits pay off in higher quality of wine grapes."[2]

Fintan du Fresne, winemaker at Chamisal Vineyards in California's Edna Valley, agreed. "At this point, the benefit to being certified sustainable is still less about selling more wine," he said. "It's about looking critically at the winery's environmental, social and economic impacts. Philosophically it's the right thing to do."[3]

Organic Food and Wine: The Globalization of Regions

Today the world has many causes for anxiety, and with the development of new technologies, we are concerned by the uncertainty of our future. Consumption of locally grown food has been part of our everyday life for centuries, but our meals today are mainly made of vegetables and other industrial or genetically modified products.

However, cultural globalization does not only mean uniformity or standardization; it also revives local, high quality production. The food revolution is a clear example of this. A growing part of the population (annual growth of 3 to 4%) is developing a "return to source" type of consumption, where food is grown locally and the seasons and environment are respected. This resurgence of local cuisine is also illustrated by fast food chains who have adapted their standard menus to seasons and local produce, to retain their clientele.

This trend is also developing in winemaking. In conventional farming, chemical fertilizers are used to produce greater yields and protect plants from disease. These same chemical products are absorbed by the roots of the vines, passing into the sap, then the leaves and finishing in the fruit. Consequently, residues of these chemicals can be found in the wines.

In addition to its effects through direct consumption, conventional farming "with chemicals" has a significant impact on the quality of soils and water. Winemakers who use chemicals must wear Hazmat-style clothing and respiratory apparatus to protect themselves when spraying.

Wine production has two main stages—the first stage is in the vines (e.g., growing the grapes) and the second is in the cellars (e.g., grape fermentation to make wine, bottling, etc.). The definition of an organic wine as "a wine made with organically grown grapes" only refers to the first stage (growing of the grapes). Many potential additions may occur during the second stage of production to ferment and preserve the wine. The most common preservative for wine is sulfur dioxide. The question of preserving wine is therefore central to the debate about the definition of organic wine.

In a few of the world's winemaking regions, grapes have been grown organically for centuries. However, organic vine growing only became widespread about thirty years ago when vine growers, faced with exhausted soils and weakened vines prone to disease, began looking for a profitable way to grow more resistant grapes.

Dubious vinification techniques may have made the first organic wines rough and unstable, but the pioneers quickly understood that organically grown grapes had a greater natural resistance to bad weather and disease and produced better results in difficult years. According to some experts, these new methods also produced sturdier grapes with more intense flavors. And the resulting wines were a more literal expression of the unique character of their regions. Indeed, in the 1980s, a few of the greatest names in wine (Chateau Margaux in Bordeaux, Domaine Leroy in Burgundy, Frog's Leap and Grgich Hills in the Napa Valley, California) adopted or were starting to adopt organic farming methods to grow the best grapes.

In the United States, changes to organic wine labeling date back to 1990, when Congress adopted the law concerning the production of organic foods to protect farmers, handlers, processors, retailers and consumers, ensuring that the foods labeled organic were indeed organic.

The law concerning the production of organic foods tasked the United States Department of Agriculture (USDA) to establish the regulations for organic foods and food products. They in turn established the National Organic Standards Board (NOSB) to advise them. As fermented drinks were included in the law concerning the production of organic foods, the Food and Drug Administration (FDA), which regulates wine labeling, was also involved. The National Organic Program (NOP), also part of the USDA, joined their ranks. The NOP's remit was to establish regulations for processing and labeling organic products, and to draw up the national list of authorized and banned substances.

Following on the equivalence arrangements signed by the United States and the European Union, this study of the paradoxes of organic wine, focusing essentially on France and California (representing 87% of American organic vines), will help one understand regulations, improve market knowledge and provide an international overview of organic wine, whether you want to produce, sell or buy, because, according to Britt and Per Karlsson (Biodynamic, Organic and Natural Winemaking), "To have an opinion on whether something is good or bad, you need first of all to understand what it means."[4]

The leading four markets for "organic" wine (or wines "made with organic grapes") are France, Germany, the United Kingdom and the United States.

The Main European Markets
Germany: The Market for Organic Food

Germany is the biggest market in Europe for organic food and second largest in the world. The German organic food market reached 7.91 billion euros in 2014 according to data from Biofach 2015 (+4.8 % compared to 2013 but +12% from consumers under 30 years of age). According to the recently published report by TechSci Research, Germany's organic food market grew strongly in 2014 with a rate of 9 % above all other kind of distribution channels and is projected to grow another 9% during 2015–19 in value terms. It has developed considerably over the last ten years. In 2000, sales stood at only 2.05 billion euros to reach 2.74 billion euros in 2014 which represents a growth of 44% since 2010. The organic market represents 4% of the entire food market (3.5% in 2009).

According to a 2015 BioFach study, supermarkets represent 53% of the organic market while specialized stores represent 33%. Discount chains are an important retail channel for organic products in Germany.

Organic alcoholic beverages are one of the organic products which developed the most in 2014. They represent:

- 4.9% of organic food sales,

- 1.8% of the entire market of alcoholic beverages.

Germany is the second largest market in the world for organic wine. It reached 755 million euros in 2013.

TABLE 1. The organic wine market in Germany (excl. ex-cellar sales)

	2008	2009	2010	2012	2013	2014
Sales (M€)	157	180	200	704	755	791
Annual growth		14.60%	11.00%	3.52%	7%	4.8%

Source: BioFach 2/28/2015, "News from the German organic market"

Only 15% of demand is satisfied by domestic production. Germany is the number one destination for organic wines in the EU. Light red wines are the most purchased organic wines in Germany.

In 2009, supermarkets and discount chains have become the leading retail channel for organic wines (38%). They have developed their range of organic wines and won market share versus specialized stores.

Italy: A Booming Organic Market

Italy is enjoying very dynamic growth of the organic market. The sale of organic products has been rising for nine years and is continuing its trajectory. According to data from the Italian Food Industry Services Institute (ISMEA), in 2013, sales of organic food and drink had risen by 12% while conventional food had dropped by 1.4% over the same period. The recession is, therefore, not affecting the Italian organic market. (At the time of this writing, 2014 numbers were not yet official. But preliminary projections reflect the trends reported herein.)

In terms of value, the current assessment of Italy's consumption of organic products stands at 3 billion euros. The European market as a whole is estimated at 18.4 billion euros. This means that to date, Italy is one of the leading producing and exporting countries in the world, as well as the second largest organic farming area in Europe (over 1.15 million hectares) after Spain (1.59 million hectares).

This excellent organic market is also illustrated by the fast growth of the number of processing factories, resellers and importers of organic products. The number of importers climbed 30% in 2012. This dynamic energy is affirmed by two-figure growth in sales of biscuits, confectionery and snacks (+22%), fruit and vegetables (+14.6%) and eggs (+11.3%). The increase in sales of dairy products is the most moderate (+0.5%) but cheese and other dairy products still generate around 18% of sales of organic foods.

The growth in organic farming is challenging the recession suffered by the primary sector. A new farming network is establishing itself with a rural economy based on small non-standard farms and collective structures such as self-managed cooperatives and consortia. Distribution organization has resulted in a proliferation of local markets with schedules published on organic websites and in local newspapers, in collaboration with local associations that are multiplying their activities in parallel with the "glocal" environmental perspective. The greatest representative of the food revolution movement is Carlo Petrini, voted a "Champion of the Earth" in September 2013 by the UN. He founded the Slow Food organization and has been running it since 1989. In 2004, he launched Terra Madre, a network of food communities committed to producing sustainable food. In the same trend, Tenuta San Guido in Tuscany, which is one of the largest producers of wine from Bolgheri and known around the world, displayed organic practices on its website (http://www.tenutasanguido.com). The entire organization of the property is considered generally nature friendly; from horse breeding to birds' pond, it became a natural reserve through the cultivation of cereals practiced through crop rotation.

Consumers of organic food can mostly be found in the north of the country and generally have a healthy standard of living and good education. But according to the latest census by the National Farming Business Institute (INEA), regions in southern Italy have surpassed those in the north in terms of the number of farmers and the total area farmed. Most organic farmers can now be found in Sicily, Calabria and Apulia. If we add the farms in Latium, Sardinia, Marches, Campania, Abruzzo and Basilicata, southern and central Italy total 61% of all working farmers. In terms of the size of the farmed area,

Sicily and Apulia alone represent over a quarter of the peninsula's organic agricultural land.

Spain: A Promising Market

While prices and volumes are dropping throughout the food sector, sales of "organic" food rose by 20% in 2011 and continued to grow at the same pace in 2012, according to figures provided by the organizers of the BioCultura trade fair that takes place every year in Barcelona.

The "organic" food segment seems to be one of the rare markets unaffected by the recession in Spain: The 7th European market for consumption of ecological and organic products, Spain should enjoy 12% growth until 2020 to reach 12,182 million euros.

Spain ranked 5th in the world in terms of organic farming with over 1.6 million hectares farmed in 2012, boosted by 84,000 hectares in 2013, according to a study released in February 2015 by Vitisphere.com. Spain showed in 2014 an impressive growth rate in acreage converted to organic since 2008: +172%. Meanwhile, organic product consumption per capita is still modest at: €21.50, but more than 2009's €19.40. Despite the largest European organic supermarkets, Spain's domestic market is restricted. It is the anomaly of the Spanish Organic Wine market: Spain produces 27% of the world's organic wine in 2014, but the country's wine drinkers consume only 1% of that production.

Spanish organic products are heavily exported: 80 to 85% of Spanish organic resources are exported and processed elsewhere, according to the General Secretary of Fepeco (Spanish Federation of Business in Organic Products), José María González Vitón, even if local organic industry is slowly taking shape. Veritas supermarkets are leaders on this market, having first appeared in Catalonia in 2002.

United Kingdom: An Organic Market in Decline

The United Kingdom's sales of organic produce have risen for the first time in four years in the UK, by 4% in 2014, but the increase was not felt across wines sales at supermarkets, where they tumbled 7.6%, according to a study conducted by the Soil Association published in February 2015. The organic market comprises around 0.2% of the overall wine market, and it is worth around £9 million. "However," Lee Holdstock, Soil Association Trade Development manager, "there is evidence of a recovery in the 12 weeks to the end of January 2015, up 2.5% and the picture seems to be improving"[5]

Similarly to organic food, supermarkets are the main channel for organic wine sales. In 2013, organic products represented 1.95% of the entire British food market. The main retail chains selling organic wines are Tesco, Sainsbury's, Asda and Morrisons. They represented over 70% of the market in 2014. The main organic retailer in terms of market share per the Soil Association 2014 report was Sainsbury, with 29% of sales in chain stores in 2013. The other main chains on the United Kingdom's organic market were: Waitrose (25.3%), Asda (8.7%) and Morrisons (6.8%).

Pinot Gris, Sauvignon Blanc and red wines from Spain, Italy and the South of France are the main types of organic wines consumed in the United Kingdom.

The organic market in the UK represented £1.86 billion in sales in 2014 which corresponds to a growth of 4% from 2013 but a decline since 2011. In 2012, organic sales fell by 1.5% and in 2013 they stumped by 3.7% according to a study published in the Guardian in March 2014.

The main reason for this decline is the country's economic situation. Families are still trying to save money on household expenses. Chain stores have also reduced their organic ranges and shelf space over the last few years.

The French Market: An Established Demand for Organic Food

In France, the organic food market was estimated at 4.59 billion euros at the end of 2014, with:

- €4.38 billion (+9% from 2012) spent by households,
- 172 million (+1.8% from 2012) spent by collective catering.

This market grew four-fold between 1999 and 2011, growing 120% between 2007 and 2013.

TABLE 2. The organic food market in France (€M)

1999	2005	2007	2008	2009	2010	2011	2012	2013	2014
1000	1565	2070	2606	3149	3514	3913	4189	4556	4559

Source: Agence BIO/AND-International

In 2013, organic wine sales represented 11% of the entire organic food market in France with a jump in sales of 22% totaling €503 million in sales and according to the "Agence Bio," wine is the organic produce with the biggest growth rate in the last four years: +56%.

TABLE 3. Breakdown of organic sales by category, all retail channels—2014

Fruit and vegetables	17.00%
Milk and dairy produce	14.00%
Eggs	6.00%
Wine	11.00%
Bread/flour	8.00%
Beef, lamb/mutton and pork	7.00%
Poultry	3.00%
Raw and cooked cured meats	2.00%
Seafood, cured and smoked fish	2.00%
Other beverages	5.00%
Ready meals and frozen food	25.00%

Source: Agence BIO/AND-International—July 2015

A High Demand for Organic Wines

France is the world's leading market for organic wines. The results from the 2015 Challenge Millésime Bio, the premier international organic wine competition, indicate that France dominates in term of quality. Of the competition's 39 gold medal winners in the red category, France took home 23 medals.

Organic wine sales (excluding exports) were stated at €503M in 2013. Between 2005 and 2013, sales grew 166%. (At the time of this writing, sales numbers for 2014 were not yet official. But preliminary projections reflect the trends reported herein.)According to a study by Inter Rhône (Challenges and perspectives for organic winemaking, 2010), 99% of organic wines consumed in France are domestic wines.

Organic wine is leaving its "niche" status behind. "The organic market should no longer be considered a novelty," said Elisabeth Mercier, director of the Agence Bio, a French organization committed to organic agriculture, and she goes on to explain that "The category has moved forward and is gaining traction due to positive market signals which are encouraging conversion".[6] In 2013, it represented 10% of organic food products in France, or 21.7 % growth in one year and 66% in five years. According to the latest Ipsos study initiated by Sudvinbio (Trade Association for organic wines from Languedoc-Roussillon), in the six months preceding the survey, 35% of French people had already purchased organic wine (+2 points compared to the same survey in 2011). These organic wine buyers are generally male, of above-average income and above-average education, according to the recent study. They are informed wine enthusiasts, very sensitive to the environment and organic produce.

TABLE 4. Sales of organic wine in France

	2005	2007	2008	2009	2010	2011	2012	2013
Sales (€M)	189	249	254	298	322	359	413	503
Annual growth	–	–	2.00%	17.30%	8.00%	11.50%	15.04 %	21.7%

Source: Agence Bio

Complex Distribution Channels

In 2013, 44% of French organic wine was exported, mainly to Germany, the US and Japan. When we look at the French market, 1/3 of organic sales were direct sales and 1/3 were through organic/natural grocery stores. The remainder was sold through supermarkets and wine merchants.

Supermarkets represented 19% of sales in 2013, with volumes increasing by 6.5% compared to 2012.

94% of these types of retailers sold organic wines (an average of 12 wines according to Millésime Bio - Professional Forum for Organic Winemaking, January 28, 2014).

TABLE 5. Development of the market for wine made with organic grapes in France, by retailer

	2005	2007	2008	2009	2010	2011	2013
Supermarkets	24.00%	20.00%	20.00%	19.00%	20.00%	20.00%	19.00%
Specialized organic stores	–	34.00%	34.00%	33.00%	31.00%	31.00%	25.00%
Wine merchants	–	13.00%	13.00%	13.00%	16.00%	16.00%	18.00%
Organic stores + wine merchants	33.00%	–	–	–	–	–	–
Direct sales	43.00%	34.00%	33.00%	34.00%	33.00%	33.00%	38.00%

Source, Agence BIO/ANDI 2014

The direct sales share is slightly larger for organic wine than conventional wine. In 2012, this retail channel represented €148M (36% of the organic wine market). Sales from the vineyard and at professional trade fairs and exhibitions were the two main methods used by organic winemakers to sell their wines directly.

TABLE 6. Breakdown of the main retail channels for wine directly sold by producers (number of users NU and turnover TO)

Wine	NU	TO
From the vineyard/estate	63.00%	69.00%
Exhibitions and trade fairs	13.00%	13.00%
Other markets	5.00%	4.00%
Restaurants	5.00%	3.00%
Door-to-door	4.00%	6.00%
Mail-order	4.00%	2.00%
Cooperative stores	2.00%	2.00%
Organic markets	1.00%	0.00%
CSA	1.00%	0.00%

Source, Agence Bio 2014

The American Market
Growing Demand for Organic Food

The American organic sector (food and non-food) has enjoyed regular growth over the last 10 years. According to the Organic Trade Association (OTA), in 2014, sales rose to reach nearly 42 billion dollars, the fastest growth rate in five years.

The organic food sector continues to represent the vast majority (93%) of organic products purchased by American consumers.

Over the last ten years, sales of organic food has grown faster than the conventional food market. In 2014, organic food represented over 5% of the food sales in the United States totaling 35.9 billion dollars (OTA, 2015). In 2000, it only represented 1.2%.

TABLE 7. Organic food sales in the United States per product. Beverages represented 12.1% of organic food sales in 2013 (4 billion dollars).

Fruit and vegetables	46.00%
Dairy products	15.00%
Pre-packaged meals	14.00%
Beverages	**12.00%**
Breads and cereals	11.00%
Snacks	4.00%
Condiments	2.00%
Meat, poultry and fish	2.00%

Source: Organic Trade Association's 2014 Organic Industry Survey

The same statistics from the Organic Trade Association 2015 also shows that 51% of families are buying more organic products in 2014 than the year before.

TABLE 8. Organic sales versus total sales, growth and market penetration in the United States

Category	2003	2005	2007	2009	2011	2013
Organic Food sales (millions dollars)	9,626	13,260	16,183	22,497	26,336	32,335
Growth %		19.5	19.20	16.40	4.30	9.20	11.40
% of total Organic	96.6	94.7	93.9	92.6	92.3	92.1
Organic non-food sales (millions dollars)	439	745	1,182	1,800	2,196	2,770
Growth %		20.30	32.60	25.00	9.10	11.20	12.80
% of Total Organic	4.40	5.30	6.10	7.40	7.70	7.90
Total Organic sales (millions dollars)	10,055	14,005	19,370	24,297	28,531	35,104
Growth %		19.00	19.80	16.90	4.60	9.30	11.50

Source: "2014 survey of the organic sector", Organic Trade Association, 2015

A High Demand for Organic Wines
Sales of Wine (Organic and Non-organic)

According to a survey published by the IWSR, the still wine market in the United States should be the fastest developing market in the world over the next few years.

Argentinean wines are increasingly popular. However, the greatest increase comes from Chilean wine sold cheaply and in bulk. Furthermore, the idea that regular and moderate wine consumption is good for your health is spreading, which boosts the market. Between 2009 and 2015, the market should increase by around 40 million cases.

TABLE 9. Forecast wine consumption in the United States (volumes) (All volumes are in thousands of 9 liter cases)

	2004	2009	2012	2015	% 2009-15
Still wines	248402	281205	310665	321960	14.00%
Sparkling wines	13287	14713	15535	16596	13.00%

Source: The IWSR, (International Wine and Spirit Research)

Sales of Organic Wine

There is a lack of public data specific to the organic wine market in the United States. However, the small amount of available data allow us to draw up a global estimation of the market.

A Nielsen report published in August 2015 summarized 52 weeks of data from the US organic wine market. Sales of organic wine and wine made with organic grapes totaled 83,230,000 million dollars from mid-August 2014 to mid-August 2015, a 24.50% increase to the previous 12 month period. In the words of report authors, "available data suggest that the popularity of organic wines has risen over the last few years similarly to that of other organic products."

Moreover, in a 2015 survey by the Organic Trade Association, penetration of organic drinks on the beverage market (including wine) in the United States was greater than 2.5% in recent years, compared to 1.8% in 2004. This means that sales of organic drinks have increased faster than those of conventional drinks over recent years.

Organic wines consumed in the United States are essentially domestic. Imported organic wines come for the most part from France, Italy, Spain, South America, Australia and South Africa.

The Market is Dominated by a Few Organic Wine Brands

Bonterra is by far the best selling organic wine brand in the US.

7 Deadly Zins is a relatively close second and Belle Ambiance Family Vineyard a distant third.

Mass retail (conventional supermarkets, clubs/warehouse stores and big box stores) sold majority of organic goods (around 50%) while organic and specialized stores sold a little less (around 40%)

The remaining sales occurred on the Internet, at farmers' markets, CSA (community-supported agriculture) events, exports, mail-order and specialized stores.

There are no specific data about the distribution of organic wine.

TABLE 10. The top 20 organic wines with the best sales in stores in the USA (including wines made with organic grapes and organic wines with no added sulfites)

Winery	Sales in $
Bonterra	14,800,000
7 Deadly Zins	11,000,000
Belle Ambiance Family Vineyard	8,500,000
EPPA	4,500,000
Edna Valley Vineyard	3,700,000
Grgich Hills	3,700,000
Natura	3,700,000
Our Daily Red	3,500,000
Frey	2,700,000
Earthquake	2,700,000
Pacific Redwood	1,000,000
R W Knudsen Family	1,000,000
Tilia	1,000,000
Acacia	930,000
Badger Mountain	800,000
Hahn	720,000
McFadden	720,000
Juan Gil	620,000
Calnaturale	750,000
Domaine Jean Bousquet	675,000

Source: Nielsen, all of American sales, Organic wines; 52 weeks ending 15th August 2015; volume of sales in dollars

TABLE 11. Organic grape variety sales in US dollars—change in %

Organic Wine Total	83,229,764	+ 24.5
Cabernet Sauvignon	13,273,598	+ 27.90
Chardonnay	12,455,428	+ 23.60
Other Red	11,200,995	+ 31.50
Sauvignon Blanc	8,562,967	+ 27.10
Pinot Noir	3,567,197	+ 65.60
Merlot	3,457,679	+ 11.90
Pinot Grigio	2,478,944	+ 68.90
Malbec	2,184,538	+ 20.40

Source: Nielsen, all of American grocery stores, 3 months ending 08/15/2015

Notes

1   M.Delmas, N. Nairn-Birch, M.Balzarova, *Lost in a sea of green: Navigating the eco-label labyrinth*, UCLA (2012)

2   http://www.ampeloscellars.com/scripts/cpg.cfm/10

3   http://www.chamisalvineyards.com/About-Us

4   Britt and Per Karlsson, *Biodynamic, Organic and Natural Winemaking: Sustainable Viticulture and Viniculture*, (2012), p.20

5   http://harpers.org/archive/

6   http://www.agencebio.org/communiques-et-dossiers-de-presse

CHAPTER 2
The Paradoxes of Unchecked Regulation

Consumer Confusion

Organic wine is defined as a wine made with grapes grown using organic farming which typically excludes the use of artificial chemical fertilizers, pesticides, fungicides and herbicides.

Despite the need for very stringent regulations, organic wine production is confusing if not unregulated in terms of the criteria and definitions; many certifications and labels coexist. The American consumer market has wines labeled "organic" and also wines labeled "made with organic grapes." There are also "biodynamic" wines, sustainable winemaking methods, so-called "natural" wines, pure wines and even "naked" wines.

These terms offer many choices but generate a certain confusion for consumers. There are other words, too: sustainable, eco-responsible, environmentally friendly, grown ecologically, etc. Some wine producers may farm with the greatest respect for the environment, but there are no restraints on terms such as "sustainable" or "grown ecologically."

Consumer confusion is a recurrent theme in many articles about organic wine in the American press. The problem stems primarily from the labeling. As highlighted by Paolo Bonetti in Organic Vintners, "The terms 'organic' and 'natural' are unclear to the general public. In the end, almost everything could be 'natural.'"

Red Cup Agency recently carried out an online survey with wine drinkers. It revealed that only 21% of people understood the difference between organic wine, biodynamic wine and wine produced from sustainable farming. Fifty percent said they "more or less understood" the differences. Even though 60% believed that people who eat organic food would also drink organic drinks, they were unsure of how to dissipate this confusion. They did state that an explanation on the labels would help them.

All these eco-labels and market terms are a source of confusion for consumers and even buyers. But one label is consistent: "organic." From a marketing point of view, "organic" remains the eco-label the most recognized by consumers for food and drink. It is a precious marketing advantage in the current consumer market. It protects them from the abusive use of other terms and helps them buy organic.

Eco-labels for Grapes and Wines in California

To receive the "wine of California" designation, 100% of grapes used in the wine must be grown in state. To receive a regional designation such as "Napa," "Sonoma," or "El Dorado County," 85% or more of the grapes used must be grown in the region in question.

In California fifteen years ago, there were two main environmental certifications: "organic" and "biodynamic." Today, there are many more certifications on the market, each with its own characteristics such as geographical delimitations, as we can see in the table below with "Napa Green," only available in Napa County. Some certifications allow a logo on the bottle ("SIP" and "Lodi Rules"), while the "CCSW" does not.

TABLE 12. American eco-labels and areas where they are recognized

Labels	United States	California	Regions of California	International
"100% organic" "Organic" "Made with organic grapes"	X	X	X	X
Biodynamic	X	X	X	X
Certified California Sustainable Winegrowing		X	X	
Lodi Rules		X	X	
Sustainability in practice (SIP)		X	X	
Green business program in the San Francisco Bay area			X	
Fish-friendly farming			X	
Napa Green Estate and Napa Green Winery			X	

These certifications can be divided into 3 groups

Certifications concerning the environmental impact of grape growing and/or wine production	Certifications concerning the environmental impact of grape growing and/or wine production that also take into account social and economic aspects	Certifications only concerning environmental aspects
Organic	CCSW	Fish-friendly farming
Biodynamic	Lodi Rules	Green business program in the San Francisco Bay area
Napa Green	SIP	

But these certifications all share a common objective: promoting environmentally friendly practices for grape growing and, for some of these certifications, for wine production too.

"Organic" Labels

"Organic" is a kind of environmental certification sponsored by the federal government which applies to all farm produce that meets a set of standards. There are three types of environmental certification sponsored by the federal government under the term "organic": "100% organic," "organic," and "made with organic grapes."

"100% Organic Wine"

Wine labeled, presented or sold as "100% organic" must satisfy the following criteria:

All grapes and other farmed ingredients (including yeast if it is available for retail) must be certified organic, except for those on the National List.

Non-farmed ingredients must be specifically authorized on the National List.

- There must be no added sulfur dioxide (sulfites), except for natural levels present at less than 10 parts per million.
- The yeast must be certified organic.
- The wine must not be produced on land where any prohibited substance has been applied over the 3 years immediately preceding the harvest of the farmed products.
- A history of all substances used on the land over the previous three years must be provided.

- The label of the wine can include the USDA organic seal and can be sold, labeled and presented as organic.

- The label must mention the name of the certifier (*certified organic by* *** or a similar sentence).

"Organic Wine"

Wine labeled, presented or sold as "Organic" must satisfy the following criteria:

All grapes and other farmed ingredients (including yeast if it is available for retail) must be certified organic, except for those on the National List.

- The non-farmed ingredients must be specifically authorized by the National List and the total of these ingredients cannot exceed 5 percent of the total product (excluding salt and water).

- There can be no sulfur dioxide added (sulfites).

- The yeast must be certified organic.

- The wine must not be produced on land where any prohibited substance has been applied over the 3 years immediately preceding the harvest of the farmed products.

- A history of all substances used on the land over the previous three years must be provided.

- The label of the wine can include the USDA organic seal and can be sold, labeled and presented as organic.

- The label must mention the name of the certifier (*certified organic by* *** or a similar sentence).

"Made with Organic Grapes"

Wine labeled, presented or sold as "Made with organic grapes" must satisfy the following criteria:

- 100 percent of the grapes (of all varieties) must be certified organic.

- Any other farmed ingredient (e.g., yeast) does not have to be organic, but must be produced without using anything prohibited such as most conventional pesticides and fertilizers, synthetic ingredients, ionization or sewage sludge.

- Non-farmed ingredients must be specifically authorized on the National List.

- Sulfur dioxide (sulfites) can be added up to 100 parts per million total in the wine.

- The label cannot include the USDA organic seal.

- The wine must not be produced on land where any prohibited substance has been applied over the 3 years immediately preceding the harvest of the farmed products.

- A history of all substances used on the land over the previous three years must be provided.

- The label can state "Made with organic grapes."

- The label must mention the name of the certifier (certified organic by *** or a similar sentence).

- Certifications under the term "organic"

There are two types of organic certificates:

- Production or farming certificate: certifies that the grapes, fruits or other products used in the end product were grown organically in compliance with USDA/NOP standards.

- The processing or handling certificate: certifies that the winery or installation where the end product is manufactured operates in compliance with USDA/NOP standards.

Both the producer and the handler/processor must be certified for "100% organic," "Organic" and "Made with organic grapes" labels, and the handling/processing certificate is sufficient documentation. However, export certificates are not sufficient.

In other words, certification can only take place at the vineyard or the winery; specific wines or grapes are not certified. A vineyard can decide, pending certification as an organic vineyard, to buy organic grapes from another vineyard and receive certification for the wine production, as a processor. The vineyard will adapt its operations over time, according to its processing certification while taking the necessary actions to obtain complete certification for production and processing in under three years.

Several certifications can be obtained at once. For example, vineyards and/or wineries in California can be certified "Napa Green" or "Sustainability in practice" (SIP). They can also be certified by "Lodi Rules" or approved by "Certified California Sustainable Winegrowing" (CCSW).

Requirements in Terms of Labeling Organic Wine

As well as meeting the above criteria for each certification, organic alcoholic beverages must also meet the rules of the Alcohol and Tobacco Tax and Trade Bureau (TTB), including specific demands in terms of sulfite labeling.

To ensure these regulations are respected, labels for alcoholic beverages made by a certified company must be approved according to the following stages before the sale of organic alcoholic beverages:

- The certifier examines the label(s) to check compliance with organic USDA regulations.
- The certifier stamps/signs the label(s) confirming compliance with organic USDA regulations.
- Once the permit has been obtained from the TTB, the organic company fills out a request for the Certificate of Label Approval (COLA).
- The organic company submits the COLA request and the label(s) approved by the TTB certification agent. *There is no need for a copy of the organic certification.*

A label must not state that a product is organic nor use the USDA organic seal without certification.

However, certified organic ingredients can be identified on the label if there are any (e.g., organic yeast). A copy of the organic ingredient certificate must be submitted to the TTB with the COLA request.

You will find the complete version of these regulations with a sample label for the three categories of organic wines in Appendix B.

Organic wine standards will doubtlessly change over the next five years to accept higher levels of sulfites (similar to the European Union). Apparently, the National Committee for Organic Standards which draws up recommendations for the NOP is calling for greater tolerance for sulfites on the NOP list. The old guard of winemakers who have been making organic wine for decades is vehemently opposing this change. But these new standards will very probably be adopted, and when they are, organic wine will flood the market. I cannot encourage you enough to read this twenty-page document dedicated to organic standards.

"Organic" Certifiers

There are currently 82 certifiers accredited by the USDA and authorized to certify activities according to USDA organic standards.

The California Certified Organic Farmers (CCOF), formed in 1973 and located in Santa Cruz, are the main and largest third-party certifier in the wine industry. CCOF offers organic certification according to the National Organic Program (NOP) of the USDA to farmers, cattle farmers, processors, private labelers, wine merchants and retailers.

Website: http://www.ccof.org/

The certification process below is based on the demands of the CCOF:

- The applicant contacts the certifier and receives the application dossier which contains a description of organic standards, a list of prohibited substances, the application form and the Organic System Plan. This plan is a framework document, jointly validated by the farmer and the certifier, upon which the certification is based. This plan is implemented via control practices which help verify that the plan is satisfactorily applied, that measurements and checks are made to prevent any mixing of organic and non-organic products and prohibited substances.

- The applicant returns the plan, the three-year history of substances applied to the soils and the administrative fees to the certifier, who will examine and determine if the applicant complies with organic handling and production regulations.

- If the evaluation is positive, the agent returns the evaluation along with an estimation of costs, and an on-site audit is scheduled. The inspector will check the information in the Organic System Plan and draw up a report recommending the certification or not. The applicant must provide the inspector with all documents that were mentioned in the application.

- The certifier decides to approve certification or not on the basis of an examination of the Organic System Plan and the inspector's report.

- Certification must be renewed annually. To respect this, the applicant must submit updates and corrections concerning modifications recommended by the certifier, Organic System Plan updates and annual certification costs. An inspection takes place every year.

In 2014, total costs included $325 administration fees paid only once and inspection fees which are billed by the hour ($65).

Small producers and processors are normally certified for between $600 and $1,200. Many small farmers can be certified for around $700 the first year and between $300 and $500 the following years.

Logo, Website, and Contact

Website: http://www.usda.gov/wps/portal/usda/usdahome?navid=ORGANIC_CERTIFICATIO

Agency administrator:
amsadministratoroffice@ams.usda.gov

National Organic Program:
http://www.ams.usda.gov/AMSv1.0/nop

Miles McEvoy, Deputy Administrator
Email: miles.mcevoy@ams.usda.gov
Telephone: +1 (202) 720–1413

"Biodynamic" Label

Biodynamic farming is based on principles developed in the 1920s by an Austrian philosopher, Rudolf Steiner. The Demeter Association founded in 1928 combined his practices in biodynamic farming standards to create a strict certification program. Demeter has been present in the United States since 1985 and owns the "Biodynamic" certification label.

Biodynamic Parameters

- Agronomic rules:

  — Elements required for the agricultural organization

- — Soil husbandry
- — Biodynamic preparations
- — Plant protection
- — Protection against environmental risks
- — Obligation to report
- — Storage of seeds, young plants and perennial plants
- — Residue tests
- Use of greenhouses
- Structural components
- Rules for cattle farming
- Handling and processing after harvest

"Biodynamic" and "Organic" are similar in the way that the requirements of the National Organic Program are part of the "Biodynamic" certification process; in both cases, crops are grown without chemicals or GMOs. The differences are, for example, greater controls of the volume of raw materials imported, insistence on product recycling, etc.

Furthermore, biodynamic farming is a more holistic approach where everything is seen as an interdependent living system: animals, plants and solar system. Biodynamic practices create more resistant plants, healing the earth by feeding the soils and revitalizing plants, soils and/or cattle.

Biodynamic Certification

Biodynamic certification is not given to one crop or one field; it is for the entire farm/vineyard. Grapes grown in such a vineyard are called biodynamic grapes.

The condition required to receive the "Biodynamic" certification is to meet the standards of the National Organic Program and the Standards of Biodynamic Agriculture for one year (it could be the last of the three years of transition to "Organic" farming). The process is different if the vineyard already satisfies the NOP standards, or not.

The Certification Process

- Depending on the case, a different application file will be provided by Demeter. The application must be completed and returned with the application fee. It contains a description of the practices employed in the past and a Farming Plan, with a road map to meet the Biodynamic Farming Standards.

- An inspector will visit the farm/vineyard and check all the information provided. This inspector draws up a report recommending certification (or not) with conditions and recommendations.

- The Demeter Evaluation Circle then decides on the certification and informs the applicant.

- Certification is valid for one year.

A farm/vineyard can be considered "currently converting" and mention it in its marketing documentation. This is possible when the farm/vineyard meets or is about to meet NOP standards and when Demeter certification will be obtained within the year.

Demeter requires that NOP conditions be met, but has a sister company, Stellar Certification Service, that is an accredited certifier for "Organic" certification.

By paying only once, one or both certifications can be obtained.

Labels

If a product is certified, the Demeter seal can be on the label. How the seal is used (front label, back label, no seal but the biodynamic ingredients are highlighted in the ingredient statement) depends on the level of certification and the product type.

There are two Demeter standards for wine:

- **"Biodynamic wine"**: which authorizes practically no processing, no correction to the sugar or acidity levels, no additional yeast if fermentation stops. The Demeter logo can be used on the bottle.

- **"Made with biodynamic grapes"**: which authorizes acidification, additional tartaric acid, sugar and yeast if fermentation stops. The Demeter logo cannot be used on the bottle.

Fees are $480 in the United States when applying for a new farm/vineyard, plus inspection costs. A detailed breakdown of costs is available on request.

Logo, Website, and Contact

https://www.biodynamics.com

1661 N. Water Street, Ste 307
Milwaukee, WI 53202 USA
Telephone: +1 (262) 649–9212
info@biodynamics.com
http://www.demeter-usa.org

Demeter Association, Inc.
Post Office Box 1390
Philomath, OR 97370 USA
Telephone: +1 541.929.7148
Jim Fullmer, Executive Director
Email: Jim@Demeter-USA.org

CERTIFIED
BIODYNAMIC®

Certified California Sustainable Winegrowing (CCSW)

Launched in January 2010 and based on the statewide Sustainable Winegrowing Program (SWP) developed by the California Sustainable Winegrowing Alliance (CSWA) and the Wine Institute on the basis of sustainable winegrowing codes of practice.

Program Details

The SWP defines sustainable winegrowing as growing and winemaking practices that are sensitive to the environment (Environmentally sound), responsive to the needs and interests of society at large (socially Equitable), and are economically feasible to implement and maintain (Economically feasible)—the 3 E's of sustainability.

It provides third-party verification of a cellar or vineyard:

- Adopts and implements sustainable practices on the basis of 227 good practices.
- Meets 58 preliminary criteria
- Demonstrates continuous improvement

Certification is valid for one year.

California Sustainable Winegrowing
Alliance/Certified California
Sustainable Winegrowing
http://www.sustainablewinegrowing.org

425 Market Street, Suite 1000
San Francisco, CA 94105
United States
Allison Jordan, Executive Director,
CSWA
Telephone: +1 415.356.7535
Email: ajordan@wineinstitute.org

California Association of Winegrape
Growers
http://www.cawg.org
1121 L Street, Ste 304
Sacramento, CA 95814
United States
Email: info@cawg.org
Telephone: +1 (916) 379–8995 or
+1 (800) 241–1800

Lodi Rules

The Lodi-Woodbridge Winegrape Commission established "Lodi Rules" certification in 2005.

Program Details

- Designed to encourage measurable improvements to the environment and the ecosystem, society at large and the quality of wine.

- Requires vinegrowers to follow a broad range of sustainability practices that lead to continuous improvements of their activities. A minimum number of sustainable practices must be reached.

- Certified by a third party—Protected Harvest examined and
approved these standards and ensures their respect and traceability.

- Certification is valid for one year.

Logo, Website, and Contact

Only bottles containing 85% or more grapes certified "Lodi Rules" are eligible for certification and use of the "Lodi Rules" seal on the bottle.

Wineries looking to certify their wines produced with certified fruit must undergo a traceability audit.

http://www.lodiwine.com
Lodi Winegrape Commission
2545 W. Turner Road
Lodi, CA 95242
United States
Telephone: +1 (209) 367–4727
Email: lwwc@lodiwine.com

Sustainability in Practice (SIP)

Developed by the Central Coast Vineyard Team in 2008 to monitor vineyard practices. This certification is open to vineyards and wineries throughout California.

Program Details

The "SIP" certification focuses on:

- Vineyard certification program
- Habitat preservation
- Energy and hydraulic efficiency
- Pest management
- Quality of vines and fruit
- Quality of soils, water and air
- Human resources and training
- The "SIP" seal ensures that a vine grower completed the process that controls how he grows his fruit and confirms that his wine is produced with "SIP" certified grapes.

- An independent inspector verifies that the vine grower meets requirements through an on-site audit and documentary audit.

- Certification is valid for three years.

Logo, Website, and Contact

Only bottles containing 85% or more grapes certified "SIP" are eligible for certification and use of the "SIP" seal on the bottle. Wineries looking to certify their wines produced with certified fruit must undertake a traceability audit.

http://www.sipcertified.org
5915 El Camino Real
Atascadero, CA 93422
United States
Telephone: +1 805.466.2288
Beth Vukmanic Lopez, SIP Certification Manager
beth@sipcertified.org

The Green Business Program in the San Francisco Bay Area
Program Details

This program is available to businesses. Its aim is to improve four main areas: waste reduction, water and energy conservation and pollution prevention.

- Coordinated by the ABAG and its partners (US EPA, Cal EPA and the business community) in 9 counties in California for over 20 sectors, including winemaking.

- Businesses receive a certification seal for their own town or county by satisfying stringent criteria drawn up by the California Green Business Program in the four main areas mentioned above.

- Businesses can save money in terms of energy, water and waste, and enjoy a competitive advantage in a healthier environment for their employees

Logo, Website, and Contact

http://www.greenbiz.ca.gov

Farming that Respects Water and Fauna
Program Details

- A certification program for Vineyards (like Napa, Sonoma, Mendocino, Solano, El Dorado) which are managed with an objective of restoring fish and fauna habitats and improving the water quality.

- Participants learn about management practices that help the environment and implement ecological restoration projects.

- Three agencies (the California Department of Fish and Wildlife, the RWQCB and the NMFS) provide third-party certification.

- Certification is valid for 5–7 years.

Logo, Website, and Contact

http://www.fishfriendlyfarming.org
Contact: California Land Stewardship Institute
550 Gateway Dr. Suite 108
Napa, CA 94558
United States
Telephone: +1 (707) 253-1226
Email: info@fishfriendlyfarming.org

Napa Green—Napa Valley Vineyards: An Example of Organic Strategy
Program Details

Focused on environmentally sound practices that achieve or exceed 20 local, Californian and federal "good practices" for agriculture and production. Open to all Vineyards and wineries in Napa County.

2 certification programs:

Certified Napa Green Vineyard

- In partnership with the FFF, the Napa County Agricultural Commissioners' Office of Pesticide Regulation and the RWQCB.

- Aims to restore, protect and reinforce the regional water basin

- The "Napa Green Vineyard" certification is valid 5 years

Certified Napa Green Winemaker

- Founded in 2007 on the basis of the Green Business Program of the San Francisco Bay area and developed in coordination with the Napa Environmental Management Department.

- Group of green and sustainable business practices specific to Napa, developed for wineries who are focused on sustainable practices, from vines and soils to winemaking in the cellars.

- "Napa Green Winemaker" certification is valid 3 years

Logo, Website, and Contact

http://www.napagreen.org
Napa Valley Office
P.O. Box 141
St. Helena, CA 94574
United States
Telephone: +1 707–963–3388
reception2@napavintners.com
Heather Butler, Executive Director

European Eco-labels
New Regulations Concerning Organic Wine Produced in the EU

Regulations concerning labeling for organic wine produced in the EU have recently changed and are published in Regulation (CE) 203/2012.

These new regulations concerning the production of organic wine introduce a technical definition of organic wine which corresponds to the organic objective and principles stated in Regulation (CE) 834/2007 of the Organic Production Council. This means that as of the 2012 harvest, only wines that respect the new European specifications concerning organic winemaking can be labeled "organic." Only vintages dated before 2012 can continue to be sold as "wine made with organic grapes."

This regulation identifies the winemaking techniques and substances authorized in organic wine. They include: a maximum sulfite content of 100 mg per liter for red wine (150 mg/l for conventional red wine), 150 mg/l for white/rosé wine (200 mg/l for conventional white/rosé), with a 30 mg/l differential for residual sugar above 2g per liter.

The new European regulations recognize that the current practice of adding sulfur to protect wine from oxidation and microbes does not stray very far from "organic" wine standards. Consequently, wines that satisfy these standards will be labeled "organic."

TABLE 13. The differences between European and American standards: Organic labeling and sulfite content for grapes grown organically and the production process for organic wine

Region	Red	White	Label
EU less than or equal to	100 mg/l	150 mg/l	Organic wine
EU more than	100 mg/l	150 mg/l	Wine made with organic grapes
USA less than or equal to	10 mg/l	10 mg/l	Organic wine
USA more than	10 mg/l	10 mg/l	Wine made with organic grapes

French Certifications
Ecocert

Ecocert is a control organization that guarantees the organic nature of wines.

France Vin Bio

Founded in 1998, the National Trade Association for Organic Wines (FNIVAB) became "France Vin Bio" at the end of 2013. Having supported the development of France's organic wine industry, FNIVAB also participated in European negotiations leading up to the definition of organic winemaking specifications which came into effect in 2012.

Now that the term "organic wine" has overtaken "wine made with organically grown grapes," the National Trade Association is also updating itself. It federates several regional trade associations: SudVinbio, Bio Aquitaine, Vin bio de Loire, Arbio and AIVABAC (Champagne), representing half of the organic winemakers in France.

It supported the development of France's organic wine industry through its participation in European negotiations on the definition of organic winemaking specifications. France Vin Bio's missions are also:

- Defense and promotion of organic wines (AB certified) at trade fairs and exhibitions, particularly through negotiating special participation deals for members of the Charter,

- Promotion of the Vin Bio FNIVAB Charter, its clear presentation, regional implementation, provision of traceability documents associated with the Charter,

- Publication of news associated with organic wines, particularly the publication of a monthly technical newsletter and the organization of "organic wine" forums in various regions,

- Management of the Charter, the Regional Charter Audit Commissions and Technical Commissions on current oenological subjects,

- Statistics reporting (Agence BIO).

Exporting Organic Food

In general, organic products that satisfy trade agreement conditions can be exported to the following markets:

- Canada

- European Union (EU)

- Japan

- Taiwan

Because we are interested in exporting American "organic" labeled wine to the European Union, we are going to examine the new European regulations on organic wine and the arrangement between the EU and the US about the labeling of organic wine.

The Equivalence Arrangement Between the US and the EU

The EU and the US have recognized their organic production rules and verification systems as equivalent in their respective regulations*. This kind of recognition is called an "equivalence arrangement."

It means that products certified organic according to USDA organic standards or EU organic standards may be sold and labeled as organic both in the US and in the EU. If the business is certified by a USDA accredited certifier or by an organization recognized by a member state of the EU, this recognition eliminates the requirement of a separate organic European certification according to American standards, and vice versa.

The European organic logo and the USDA organic seal can both be used on products sold within the framework of this arrangement.

Even though this is now an official regulation, this arrangement irritates American winemakers because their products meet stricter standards and contain less than 10 mg of sulfites per liter compared to the 100 authorized in Europe, which they see as unfair.[1]

Perception of Organic Wine and Eco-labels by American Consumers

Current trends favor a "green" wine market. Consumers reflect more on their health and are interested in the environmental impact of what they eat and drink.

The table below indicates that organic consumers are generally wine drinkers.

TABLE 14. Organic consumers are often people who buy wine

Consumers in the sustainable food segment (organic in particular) are more likely to buy several categories of food and drink.	Food and drink categories highly sought after in dollars/1000 Index HH compared to consumers who have no feelings about sustainability.
In terms of dollars, wine is high on the list.	Wine Spirits Cooked cereals Fats and oils Refrigerated fruit juices Beer Non-refrigerated fruit juices Frozen seafood Butter Coffee

Source, IRI 2007, "Survey of food and drink," 12 months ending January 2008.

---

1. In the EU, these rules are defined by Regulation (CE) n°834/2007 of June 28, 2007 concerning organic production and the labeling of organic products and revoking Regulation (CEE) n°2092/91 (JO L 189, 20/07/2007, p. 1–23) and by Regulation (CE) n°889/2008 of September 5, 2008 defining detailed rules for the application of Regulation (CE) n°834/2007 of the Council for organic production and labeling of organic produce concerning organic production, labeling and controls (JO L 250, 18/09/2008, p. 1–84).

This 2009 survey shows that 57% of wine consumers had already heard of "organic" wine, and 20% of them had already tasted it.

TABLE 15. "Green" wines—opinion panel on wine (with 900 very frequent wine drinkers)

Term	Don't know	Have heard of	Have already tried
Natural	15.00%	48.00%	23.00%
Organic	15.00%	57.00%	20.00%
Biodynamic	49.00%	42.00%	5.00%
Sustainable	39.00%	46.00%	6.00%
Green	34.00%	50.00%	8.00%

Source: Full Glass research institute, 2009

Laura Klein, editor of Organic Authority, explains that people who eat organic food would also be likely to drink organic, natural or sustainable wine. It would be a natural addition to their lifestyle.

In 2010, Wine Business carried out a survey with 321 wine drinkers to determine how they perceive organic wine in relation to the environment. They were divided into 3 groups:

1–organic wine consumers

2–occasional organic wine consumers

3–non-organic wine consumers

When we asked them if protecting the environment was important, they all replied that yes, it was an important objective and principle. When organic wine consumers clearly declared that organic food purchases had an impact on environmental protection, non-organic wine consumers did not see the connection between the two and therefore saw little or no reason to change their behavior.

TABLE 16. I believe that by buying organic products I have a positive impact on the environment.

Non-organic wine consumer	Occasional organic wine consumer	Organic wine consumer
2.27	2.68	2.92

Opinion on positive environmental impact.
Scale: 1 = Strongly disagree, 2 = Disagree, 3 = Agree, 4 = Strongly agree

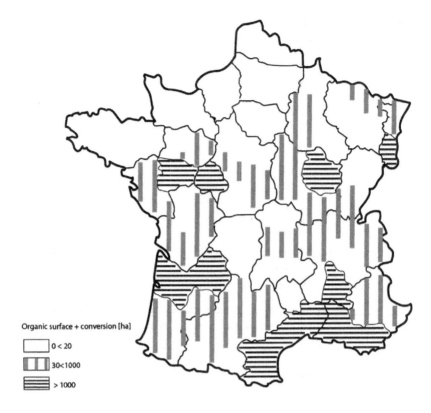

FIGURE 1.   Organic vines in France

Source: Agence BIO France

This survey also showed that organic wine buyers were more likely to believe that organic products are better for their health. However, all wine drinkers from the sample consider wine to be good for their health whatever the situation.

Chapter 3
A Paradoxically Productive and Expanding Agriculture

Organic winemaking is not an artisan niche, despite being a low percentage of the world's total vineyard area. On the contrary, it is stepping away from pre-conceived ideas of food-producing agriculture and turning toward production focused on quality, but with clear objectives in terms of exports and quantity.

According to data from the French agency Agence Bio published in January 2014, organically managed vineyards cover 273,210 hectares, +11% since 2011. Globally, organic vines represented 3.6% in 2013: 256,000 hectares (633,000 acres) out of 7.5 million hectares (18.5 million acres) of vines planted all over the world.

The vineyard area has grown significantly between 2004 and 2013, from 172,000 hectares to 273,210 hectares over this period, or +197% in seven years. These figures take into account AB certified vines and areas currently being converted.

Europe represents 90% of the world's organic vines. The main organic wine producers are:

- in Europe: Spain, France and Italy (75% of the world's wines)
- outside Europe: the United States (5%)

All these figures do not take into account all of the many and growing producers who practice biodynamics but are not certified as such. Indeed, certification appears to them more as a negative constraint than an asset. It seems that it is often expensive, does not give them an added value on their reputation (for example, classified vintages already have sufficient commercial aura) and, finally, what it requires from their production processes and administrative management seem to them too unnecessary. But the approach of a friendly production environment is increasingly at the heart of winemaking practices.

Europe: The Majority of Organic Vineyards

In 2012, over 228,000 hectares, almost 563,400 acres (around 180,000 hectares in 2010, 444 790 acres) of organic wine grapes were grown in the European Union.

In 2012, European organic vineyards were mainly in Spain (37%), France (28%) and Italy (24%). Germany and Greece each represented 3% of organic vines in Europe. Of all European Vineyards, 5.1% were organic.

Spain: The Largest Organic Vineyard

According to the International Organization for Wine and Vine (OIV), in 2014, Spain had the largest organic vineyard in Europe (and the world) with over 1.02 million hectares of organic vines, 700 wineries. Organic vines represented 11.1% of the country's organic farming. And 8.4% of Spanish vineyards were organic in 2012, an impressive growth of +373% since 2002.

Nine-tenths of organic wine production was exported, mainly to Germany, the Netherlands and the United States. Organic wines consumed in Spain represent only 0.6% of the total consumption.

MAGRAMA (Spanish Ministry of Agriculture, Food and the Environment) data indicates that there are currently nearly 700 wineries in Spain that produce organic wines—up from 135 in 2001—with the largest number concentrated in Castile-La Mancha (the largest surface area in the world dedicated to vineyards), followed by Region of Murcia, Catalonia, Valencian Community. (Adrienne Smith, "Spanish Wines go Organic," September 2015. http://www.foodswinesfromspain.com)

Italy: A Growing Organic Vineyard

In 2013, Italy was the third largest organic vineyard in the European Union, behind Spain and France with over 57,000 hectares (141,700 acres) (+9% compared to 2012). Of conventional vineyards, 36% were converting to organic farming methods. Of all Italian vineyards, 7.9% were organic in 2012. Italy boosted its organic vineyard area by 68,000 hectares in 2014 and showed an impressive growth rate of +68% in acreage converted to organic since 2008.

Sicily is the leading wine-producing region in Italy (1/3 of organic Italian vineyards). Apulia, Tuscany and Marches are the main other regions producing organic wine.

Over 50% of Italian production was exported in 2014, mainly to Germany, Switzerland the United States, Japan, the United Kingdom and Australia.

Germany: A Growing Vineyard

Germany had the fourth largest crop land planted to organic wine grapes in the European Union in 2012, with almost 7,400 hectares (18,300 acres). That's 7.6% of the country's total vineyard land (compared to 5.2% in 2010).

TABLE 17. Organic vineyard area in Germany (hectares)

2008	2009	2010	2011
4400	4700	5400	6900
	6.80%	14.90%	27.80%

France's Wine Industry: One of the Most Dynamic Organic Sectors

In 2012, 8.2% of French vineyards were organic and 38% converting to organic farming methods. Nevertheless, in 2013 France boosted its organic acreage by 64,000 hectares, an impressive growth of +188% since 2007. This represented 64,800 hectares (160,120 acres) in total. (At the time of this writing, 2014 numbers were not yet official. But preliminary projections reflect the trends reported herein.)

Organic vines represent one of the most dynamic organic agricultures in France: between 2007 and 2011, the number of vineyards grew three-fold and the vineyard area converting to organic farming represented 38% of the total organic wine grapes in 2012 (1 ha = 2.47 acres) (see Figure 1.)

Languedoc-Roussillon (20,830 hectares, 51,471 acres), Provence-Alpes-Côte d'Azur (14,285 hectares, 35,298 acres) and Aquitaine (9,732 hectares, 24,048 acres) represented over 70% of the total vineyard area using organic practices (certified + converting) and 58% of organic wine producers.

Including the area effectively converting to organic agriculture, the total area of French organic vineyards has tripled in the past five years.

The number of "AB" certified bottles (75cl) produced in France was estimated at 77 million (577,500 hl) in 2012, and at 172 million (1.29 million hl) including the converting vineyards (+50 million bottles compared to 2011).

According to the 2010 Agricultural Census, the breakdown of wines produced organically in France was (in % of harvested volumes):

Red wine: 56% (compared to 45% for conventional red wines)

Rosé wine: 18% (compared to 12% for conventional rosé wines)

White wine: 26% (compared to 43% for conventional white wines)

Thierry Julien, organic winemaker since 1989 with the AVA Coteaux du Languedoc and president of the Association Interprofessionnelle des Vins Biologiques-Languedoc Roussillon (AIVB-LR), said in an interview in January 2013 that he was expecting "high growth in the volume of certified organic wines over the next 2–3 years," because of the recent changes to the European regulations.

> From 2012 on, we will have organic wine rather than wine 'made from organically grown grapes,' Thierry Julien explains, "and French producers looking for new buyers for their products, particularly in the United States and Germany.[7]

Indicating trend in the market, even cognacs are now produced organically. Hardy Cognac VSOP Organic is a variation of the VSOP line.

Organic Viticulture Enjoys Growth in the US

The number of organically certified vineyards in the United States (for all kinds of grapes: raisins, grape juice, fruit and wine) has increased considerably over the last ten decade. In fact the vineyard area increased two and a half times over the past ten years representing more than 3.5% of the total vineyard area compared to 2.4% in 2005

TABLE 18. Increase in organically certified vineyard area in the United States (acres)

2000	2001	2002	2003	2005	2006	2007	2008	2011	2014
12575	14532	16018	21041	22800	22721	24353	28289	31771	27281

Source, USDA 2014 Census of Agriculture, Organic Survey 9/2015

According to the recent USDA Organic survey published in September 2015, in the US certified organic grapes are mainly produced in California, which, in 2014, represented 87% of the total area of organic wines (27,779 acres). California is a world leader in sustainable winegrowing practices. As of the end of 2014, nearly 80 wineries and 308 vineyards in California have been certified organic.

TABLE 19. Area of organically certified vines in the United States by State, 2014

California	Washington	Oregon	Other states
87.00%	6.00%	6.00%	1.00%

Source, USDA Organic survey, 9/2015

California Certified Organic Farmers (CCOF) certifies around 90% of organic wine grape vineyards in California. CCOF acreage doubled between 2005 and 2010. However, in the three years from 2012 through 2014, there's a not insignificant decrease in certified acreage.

TABLE 20. Area of organic wine grape vines certified by CCOF in California (acres), 2014 (1 acre = 0.4 hectare)

	2005	2006	2007	2008	2009	2010	2011	2012	2013	2014
Vine area	7761	8370	9240	9722	10318	11892	11906	11514	11237	10766
Growth rate		8.00%	10.00%	5.00%	6.00%	15.00%	0.00%	–3.30%	–2.4%	–4.19%

Source: CCOF, 2015

Around 40% of the organic vines are located in Mendocino County. Napa County is the second largest producing region (around 20%). The other organic vineyards are in Tulare, Sonoma, Santa Barbara, Amador and Fresno.

Certified "Organic" Vineyards

In July 2015, 66 US wine companies (2,800 acres) were Demeter certified "Biodynamic" for their vineyard and/or wine. A total of 44 companies are in California, with an estimated 1,950 acres.

Certified "Napa Green" Vineyards

In 2014, 61,000 acres are currently committed to the "Napa Green Vineyard" program and over 35,000 acres are certified (50 certified Vineyards); thousands of others are about to receive their official certification.

In comparison, in 2009, 27,000 acres were committed to this program, of which 13,000 were certified, which shows an increase of more than 50% between 2009 and 2014.

Certified "Lodi Rules" Vineyards

26,000 acres were certified in 2012 (15,000 acres in 2010), of which 20,000 are in the Lodi appellation area, designated an American federal viticultural region and located to the east of San Francisco, on the edge of the Sacramento Delta.

This represents around 50 wineries, 20 of which produce wines that have the "Lodi Rules" seal on the bottle.

Certified "Sustainable In Practice" Vineyards

In 2014, there were nearly 32,000 acres of "SIP" certified vines (11,000 in 2009) and over 1,350,000 cases with the "SIP" seal.

156 vineyards were certified, 53 of which were in San Luis Obispo County and 39 in Monterey.

"Certified California Sustainable Winegrowing" Vineyards (CCSW)

TABLE 21. Participants in the "Certified California Sustainable Winegrowing" program (as of November 2014)

Number of certified businesses	69
Total number of certified wineries	77
Total number of certified vineyards	215
Total number of certified acres in California (14.22% of the entire 570,000 acres in California)	81,043

Source: CCSW

Certified Organic Wine Grape Growers in California
Number of Organic Producers

In June 2015, around 444 organic wine grape growers were established in California which represent a total of 97,511.26 acres of CCSW-Certified vineyards (17.15% of the 570,000 total California acres) and a total of 157.32 million wine cases produced by CCSW-Certified wineries (65.55% of the 240 million cases produced in California).

TABLE 22. Organic wine grape growers in California

2005	2006	2007	2008	2009	2011	2015
137	135	174	206	224	259	444

Sources: California Sustainable Winegrowing Alliance, July 2015.

BV   Big Valley
CC   Central Coast
DV   Desert Valley
FT   Fresno/Tulare
HT   Humboldt/Trinity
KE   Kern
ME   Mendocino
NC   North Coast
NV   North Valley
PS   Pacific Southwest
SC   South Coast
SL   San Luis Obispo
SG   Sierra/Gold
YO   Yolo

FIGURE 2.   California chapters of CCOF.

Data Concerning Organic Wine Grape Growers—Methodology

As stated previously, the CCOF (California Certified Organic Farmers) certifies around 90% of organic wine grape vineyards in California.

All the data mentioned in the following paragraphs is based on the directory of CCOF members available from their website: http://www.ccof.org/directory

In our statistics, we have taken into account all producers of "(wine) grapes" and/or specific varieties of grapes such as "(Pinot Noir) grapes," "(Merlot) grapes," "(Cabernet Sauvignon) grapes,"etc. We have not included "(table) grapes," "(grape juice) grapes," "(raisins) grapes," or "grape" growers.

The CCOF directory currently lists 266 certified organic wine grape growers in California. You will find the list of certified organic wine producer members of the CCOF in Appendix A.

Californian Chapters

All CCOF certified members based in California belong to chapters based on their geographical areas (see Figure 2).

There are 13 CCOF chapters (of which two have been dissolved) where organic wine grapes are grown:

1. **Big Valley (BV):** Contra Costa, Merced, San Joaquin and Stanislaus Counties.

2. **Central Coast (CC):** Alameda, Monterey, San Benito, San Mateo, Santa Clara, Santa Cruz and San Francisco Counties.

3. **Fresno-Tulare (FT):** Fresno, Kings, Madera, Mariposa, Mono and Tulare Counties.

4. **Humboldt-Trinity (HT):** Humboldt, Del Norte and Trinity Counties.

5. **Kern (KE):** Kern County.

6. **Mendocino (ME):** chapter dissolved

7. **North Coast (NC):** chapter dissolved

8. **North Valley (NV):** Butte, Glenn, Lassen, Modoc, Plumas, Shasta, Sierra, Siskiyou, Tehama and Yuba Counties.

9. **Pacific Southwest (PS):** Desert Valley, Imperial, South Los Angeles, Orange, Riverside, San Bernardino and San Diego Counties.

10. **San Luis Obispo (SL):** San Luis Obispo County.

11. **Sierra Gold (SG):** Alpine, Amador, Calaveras, El Dorado, Nevada, Placer and Tuolumne Counties.

12. **South Coast (SC):** Santa Barbara, Ventura and North Los Angeles Counties.

13. **Yolo (YO):** Colusa, Sacramento, Solano, Sutter and Yolo Counties.

Organic wine grapes are mostly grown in two regions in California: Mendocino and North Coast. These two regions represent 73% of CCOF members.

Size of the Vineyards

The average size of organic wine grape properties is 74 acres.

The average size varies depending on the area/chapter. In the four main areas where organic wine grapes are grown, the average size of properties goes from 121 acres in the Fresno-Tulare region to 52 acres in the North Coast region. Average sizes in the Mendocino and Central Coast chapters are similar at around 80 acres.

TABLE 23. Producers per CCOF chapter

Chapter	Number of producers	% total
Big Valley	6	2.3
Central Coast	17	6.4
Fresno-Tulare	14	5.3
Humboldt-Trinity	3	1.1
Kern	2	0.7
Mendocino	77	28.9
North Coast	117	44
North Valley	4	1.5
Pacific Southwest	6	2.3
San Luis Obispo	4	1.5
Sierra Gold	7	2.6
South Coast	7	2.6
Yolo	2	0.7
Total	**266**	**100**

Source: California Certified Organic Farmers, 2015

TABLE 24. Average vineyard size

Chapter	Average vineyard size (acres)	Number of producers
Big Valley	45	6
Central Coast	86	17
Fresno-Tulare	121	14
Humboldt-Trinity	29	3
Kern	1115	2
Mendocino	78	77
North Coast	52	117
North Valley	87	4
Pacific Southwest	81	6
San Luis Obispo	45	4
Sierra Gold	64	7
South Coast	40	7
Yolo	13	2
Total	**74**	**266**

Source: California Certified Organic Farmers, 2015

The size also varies greatly from one property to the next:

- 45 Vineyards (17%) are under 5 acres
- 64 Vineyards (24%) are between 6 and 15 acres
- 69 Vineyards (26 %) are between 16 and 40 acres
- 46 Vineyards (17 %) are between 41 and 100 acres
- 34 Vineyards (13 %) are between 101 and 387 acres
- 8 Vineyards (3%) are over 500 acres

The two largest properties are in the Kern area, with Sunview Vineyards (2,181 acres), and the Mendocino area, with Fetzer Vineyards (1,841 acres).

Grape Varieties and Other Products

64% of organic wine grape growers in California are specialized in this production and grow one or several grape varieties.

The other estates (36%) grow wine grapes and also other products such as olives, walnuts, vegetables and fruits (including "grapes").

27 grape varieties are grown organically in California. The four main varieties, grown on over 35 estates, are Cabernet Sauvignon, Zinfandel, Merlot and Chardonnay.

TABLE 25. Grape varieties grown

Varieties	Number of estates growing this variety
Cabernet Franc	12
Cabernet Sauvignon	66
Carignan	18
Centurion	1
Chardonnay	35
Chenin Blanc	1
Colombard	4
Gewurztraminer	2
Grenache	13
Marsanne	1
Merlot	36
Mourvèdre	8

Varieties	Number of estates growing this variety
Muscat	5
Nebbiolo	3
Petit Verdot	14
Petite Syrah	27
Pinot Noir	23
Riesling Blanc	2
Roussanne	4
Ruby Cabernet	2
Sangiovese	11
Sauvignon Blanc	31
Sémillon	3
Syrah	26
Viognier	11
Zinfandel	38
Grapes (wine)	154

Notes

7   http://www.winepaper.fr/millesime-bio-interview-de-thierry-julien-et-bilan-2012-2605

Chapter 4
The Cost Paradox

The Costs of Organic Vineyards

Once again, it is important to break away from the common idea that organic wine means expensive wine. It seems on the contrary not to imply higher costs for consumers, which boosts the market and encourages producers to move toward this type of production despite greater production costs.

A survey was carried out in 2010 in 58 vineyards and/or wineries in California, 37 of which were certified or committed to a sustainability/environmental program (not necessarily certified). Amongst other things, this survey's objective was to determine if there was a difference in costs when cultivating an acre of certified grapes compared to an acre of conventional grapes.

The organic grape growers unanimously declared that growing an acre of certified grapes was more expensive. They declared that costs increased from 10% to 50% when compared to conventional viticulture. However, 80% of the answers placed the cost increase at 25% or less.

The most important factor in this cost variation was the cost of labor. Half the grape growers stated that the cost of labor had "considerably" increased, and 80% said that this increase was "considerable" or "slight."

Other inputs (particularly organic fertilizers) and certification were considered further reasons for the cost increase.

Eco-labels and the Pricing Paradox

Magali Delmas, professor at the UCLA Institute for the Environment and Sustainable Development, has been studying the effects of eco-labels on Californian wines since 1999. She realized that when an eco-label—such as "made with organic grapes," "certified by the CCOF," "USDA organic" or "certified by Demeter"—appears on these wines, the prices drop. For many, "organic" wines suffer from a bad image and a bad reputation in terms of taste.

Delmas and the researcher Laura Grant published a study on "The Enigma of the wine sector" in *Business & Society* in 2010. Using a database that included 72% of wines produced in California, the authors observed that in general terms, wines produced in vineyards that use organic processes are valued at a price 13% higher than their competitors. But placing an eco-label on these wines reduces their price by 7% compared to conventional wines, and by 20% compared to non-labeled certified wines. In a further study carried out in 2012 entitled "Eco-advantage or eco-penalty? Eco-labels and quality on the organic wine market," Magali Delmas and Niel Lessem carried out an experiment with 830 participants throughout the country. The results of this survey echoed those of the first: Consumers associate eco-labels on wine with a lesser quality but feel that they are doing something good by buying a wine with an eco-label.

Those who follow the wine sector closely were not surprised by the results of this survey. Adam Morganstern, Chief Editor of *Organic Wine Journal*, wrote:

> *There are many certified organic and biodynamic wines that are fantastic, but you need to know their names because you'll find no details on their label. This generates confusion not only amongst wine drinkers but also with sommeliers, waiters and wine merchants near you. Luckily, the situation is changing. Organic and biodynamic wines are generally better perceived but until the best wine makers 'emerge from their cellar,' if I may, the results of this survey hold no surprise.*[8]

Véronique Raskin, owner of Organic Wine Company, bemoans that the results of this survey, despite their honesty, "are completely ridiculous, in particular today when every other organic product is launched with a positive advantage in the consumer's mind, compared with its conventional counterpart."[9]

In a wine business survey of wine consumers in 2010, the question of extra cost was asked. This survey illustrated that organic wine consumers were prepared to pay more to obtain organic products, while non-buyers of organic wine do not believe that organic products are worth the increase in price. This result is corroborated by other research in Europe and Australia. Consequently, to encourage non-organic wine drinkers to try "green" wines, wine marketers must remind consumers that organic wines can be bought at attractive prices compared with non-organic wines. There are many examples of organic and environmentally sound wines on the market at under $10 a bottle.

Can organic mean an increase in price? Probably in the future, but long-term recognition for great organic wines is required, similar to the recognition of *Grand Crus*.

Marketing Organic Wines in the US

The California Wine Institute represents over 1,000 wineries and operates the largest American wine (organic and non-organic) promotion program. Its long-term strategy is focused on demonstrating the broad range and quality of California wines to ensure that the important discounts on "organic" certified wines do not tarnish their original image. The Wine Institute maintains the serious image of well-established brands and the quality of high-end wine stores but it also focuses on developing the image and availability of the average-priced segment ($10–20\

Direct Marketing by Wine Producers

As we have seen, there has been rapid growth in the demand for organic and sustainably farmed food and drinks in the United States and elsewhere. What marketing strategy are wineries adopting?

In general terms, there is very little data about wineries and their marketing strategies. They mainly self-promote on their websites, as well as participating in trade fairs and selling their products from the estate, online, at local markets, at wine clubs and in specialized and conventional chain stores.

Product Labeling

Organically produced California wines use official logos, as mentioned above.

Many certified "organic" wineries place the organic logo on the back of the bottle, with the name of the certifier. They often add an extra label beneath the main label to highlight their eco-label.

After examining several bottles, we noticed that the words "made with organic grapes" are often placed on the front label while the "organic" logos are more likely to appear on the back.

Advertising Standards Code

In the United States, many organizations (the complete list is available here) have drawn up good practice guides for marketing and advertising alcoholic beverages. These instruments are designed to help businesses advertise in a socially responsible way. This approach also helps businesses promote moderate consumption of alcohol, and avoid targeting minors and other populations at risk.

In California, the Wine Institute has drawn up an advertising standards code which must be observed when creating a marketing plan or developing a website.

In France, the "Evin" Law followed by increasingly important constraints regulate this area drastically, tending towards prohibition rather than consumer education.

Discreet Leadership for a Few Wine Producers

According to the study "*The Enigma of the wine sector*" by Delmas and Grant, a producer can eco-certify his practices and decide not to mention the certification on his product labels. Some organizations obtain certification without informing their customers.

According to Delmas, "only a third of the certified wineries put an eco-label on their bottles, which is strange because certification is a costly process." Stranger still, "These wines are of a better quality than conventional wines. But we observed that if there is a label on the bottle, it makes the price drop below that of a conventional wine. So, even though the wine may be of a better quality according to the *Wine Spectator*, the general public will not perceive it that way." [10] Another appreciable paradox!

Frog's Leap Winery in Rutherford, California, is an example. This winery was the first in Napa to go organic and adopt organic certification, but does not want to be known by its customers as an organic vineyard. John Williams, founder of Frog's Leap Winery, explains: "We don't want to be known as Napa Valley's organic winery. Until now, there's been no advantage in marketing our wine as organic wine." The labels don't mention that the grapes are grown organically; they produce organic wine for the health and longevity of the vineyard and their employees. "The advantages of going organic are what we are used to in the wine business, where we are adopting a much longer-term investment approach. I find it very difficult to find any disadvantage to being a green business," he adds.[11]

Another example is Campovida, a certified organic farm and vineyard in the heart of Mendocino County, California. They put their eco-label at the back of the bottle. "People buy the wine because of its taste," affirms Anna Beuselinck, co-founder of Campovida, "not because of the label."[12]

Example of Advertising by Bonterra Wines

Bonterra is the top selling organic wine in grocery stores.

www.bonterra.com

All of their grapes have been grown organically since 1993

- Organic grapes produce better wine

- They use certified organic practices

- They use biodynamic farming approaches

The message promotes green practices stage by stage to make life greener. Vie Bio TV shows a series of episodes about organic wine, entertaining videos, tips and tricks, recipes and a wine club. They take part in special events and professional trade fairs.

Bonterra did not respond to our request for more information. Local agencies such as Napa Valley Vineyards were not at liberty to discuss Bonterra's marketing strategies with us.

In-store Marketing in the US

The big American supermarket chains do not specifically promote organic wine in-store. Even though they sell these kinds of products, there is generally no area dedicated to organic wines in their stores; the organic wines are with the conventional wines.

On the other hand, many natural American grocery stores (like Whole Foods and Trader Joe's) and wine merchants now sell organic wine and have a specific section dedicated to organic wine, depending on the size of the store, demand, clientele profile and the store location. Five to 15% of their wine is organic, which represents 80% of the entire retail sales of organic wine. Even though traditional wines continue to dominate the wine section, these organic zones are increasing in general demand and obtaining more shelf space. (Similarly, Kosher wines can have their own area, particularly during the High Holiday season.)

Trader Joe's

We have obtained the following information through visits to Trader Joe's on several occasions and discussions with the sales assistants:

Some Trader Joe's stores have "organic" signs above the aisles, in dedicated areas. Generally, their wines are organized by grape variety and region. But an organic section has been added in the last few years. It is a decision that depends on the location of the store and consumer demand.

These wines come from all over the world ($4–$14). Trader Joe's sells its own organic wine.

While the head office (and not the individual stores) preselects the wines and wineries with which they work, in the end it is up to the store manager (generally a wine enthusiast rather than a wine expert) who decides to sell a specific wine in his store. He knows the profile of his clientele and organizes his stock accordingly.

Whole Foods

Other stores, such as Whole Foods, use signs to indicate the organic wines in-store, in an area dedicated to organic food with wines from all over the world. Certain supermarkets have their own oenologists who select their wines.

Other Specialized Wine Stores

Other specialized wine merchants carefully categorize their wines by pedigree: "Sustainable," "Organic," "Biodynamic," etc. Only a connoisseur could master the differences between all these labels. These family-run stores can sell their wines directly to consumers and educate them about the different labels and their advantages, which is impossible in supermarkets.

Wine Clubs

Organic monthly wine clubs are increasing in popularity:

- **EcoVine Organic Wine Club:** EcoVine Club is focused on customization and offers a range of organic wines including biodynamic and vegan wines. They also have a club for enthusiasts of sulfite-free organic wines and a club for aficionados of high-end organic wine from top-flight wineries.

- **The Organic Wine Company monthly wine club:** The members of this multi-functional club can choose from several variations on 3 bottles for $49.99 or the VIP club.

- **PureVineWines monthly wine club:** Managed by three wine enthusiasts in Portland, Oregon, this club enables its members to taste an assortment of organic, biodynamic and sustainably grown wines from boutique producers all over the world.

- **Organic Wine Exchange wine club:** Monthly or quarterly shipments from this club are adapted to your personality. You will receive a selection of organic and biodynamic wines from, for the most part, American and international family-owned vineyards.

- **The Organic Wine Press monthly wine club:** This organic wine merchant in Bandon, Oregon, also ships wine to its club members all over the United States.

Promotional Events in the US
California Promotes Organic Wine

The CCOF, California's main certification body, organized an organic awareness campaign called "Why buy certified organic wine?" in June 2012 as part of their continuous efforts to educate and inform consumers, helping buyers and restoring confidence.

"We want consumers to know that when they see a CCOF or USDA certified organic logo, they are buying products that really are organic because our farmers must follow strict, verifiable practices to be able to use the label."[13] (Santa Cruz, California (PRWEB), June 28, 2012)

California Restaurant Month

In California, over 3,600 wineries and 400 specialized farms take part in the California restaurant month (January) during which world-renowned wine and food take center stage with set-price gourmet dinners, wine and food pairings, events with famous chefs and exclusive seasonal offers in over 30 exceptional destinations throughout the entire state.

"California Wines: Down to Earth Month" (Every Year in April)

A movement for promoting good wine practices has generated many events across California. The Wine Institute created "California Wines: Down to Earth Month," a month-long, statewide celebration of California's leadership in sustainable winegrowing and winemaking, featuring practices that are environmentally and socially responsible. April 2014 marked the campaign's third year.

The Down to Earth Month includes a huge choice of events for visitors to get the best from this wine festival:

In Napa, Down to Earth with "Napa Green" Certified Wineries is a fun way to learn about green design, conservation and creative re-use as well as attend related tasting events. (March)

San Luis Obispo County's FarmFest on the Coast (April) offers local, sustainably grown wine and food at Dinosaur Caves Park overlooking the ocean at Pismo Beach.

Central Coast Wineries are offering an Earth Day Food & Wine Festival (April) with more than 200 growers, vintners and chefs serving local wine and food with music, dancing and more.

The Santa Cruz Mountains Winegrowers Association Passport Day celebrates its earth-friendly wine region with organic wine trails, barrel samples and special tasting flights in April. This event helps support "Save Our Shores," a non-profit association dedicated to clean beaches.

Livermore Valley wineries are highlighting sustainable winegrowing and winemaking with special "Down to Earth" tours and tastings (April).

Mendocino Wineries are offering "Where the Earth is First Fest" in April. Visitors will enjoy a host of eco-friendly activities and enjoy organic wine and food.

From April 1–30 in Northern Sonoma County, the Green Trail of Dry Creek Valley offers a special, customized experience exploring the region's certified organic and certified biodynamic wineries.

You can watch new videos about sustainability in California wine produced by the Wine Institute on www.discovercaliforniawines.com.

Professional Wine Trade Fairs and Special Events in the US and Around the World

- Unified Wine and Grape Symposium in Sacramento, California (annual, January) is the largest event of its kind in the western hemisphere. It is organized with the joint input of vineyards, wineries and allied industry members.

- Millésime bio (22nd edition January 2015 in Montpellier, France) with a long list of exhibitors that increases sales year on year.

- Prowein in Düsseldorf, Germany (in March every year) is an international wine and spirit fair.

- Vinitaly in Verona, Italy (in April every year) is an international wine and spirit fair.

- The London Wine Fair, United Kingdom (annual, May) focuses on new wines and spirits, new producers, emerging countries and regions, new crus, seminars, debates and master classes.

- Vinexpo in Bordeaux, France, in June every other year (next event June 2017) is a huge international exhibition for wines and spirits. The fringe festival for organic vintners (2,350 professionals and 48,500 visitors in 2015) was created in 2001 by Nicolas Joly (owner of the Clos de la Coulée de Serrant) in the Loire Valley.

You will find the complete list of professional trade fairs and special events for 2015 and 2016 in the United States and the world in Appendix C.

Professional Publications and Specialized Websites in the US

There is no data available about advertising for organic wines, but here are a few of the main professional magazines and websites specializing in wine:

Specialized Websites
The Organic Wine Exchange

An educational site and a sales platform for everything associated with organic and biodynamic wines.

https://organicwineexchange.com/

The Organic Wine Journal

An online guide dedicated to organic, biodynamic and natural wine.

http://www.organicwinejournal.com/

The Main Professional Publications in the US
Wine Spectator

Published 15 times a year, the *Wine Spectator* offers an exciting view of a rich lifestyle, with refined meals, wine tours and entertainment. With 2.8 million readers (source: MRI), *Wine Spectator* reaches company directors, trend-setters, epicureans and connoisseurs.

http://www.winespectator.com/

Wine Enthusiast

Published 14 times a year since 1988, this magazine created by Adam and Sybil Strum boasts 800,000 readers. It comes with an online catalog and promotes national events celebrating wine and food in major American cities.

http://www.winemag.com/

Wines and Vines

Monthly publication *Wines & Vines* focuses on subjects associated with vine growing, viticulture and wine marketing for the North American sector, with features on regions and boutique wineries. Combined paper and online circulation: 159,000:

http://www.winesandvines.com/

Beverage Information Group

Publishes annual reports on the sales and consumption of alcoholic beverages, including trends, sales of different brands, advertising expenditure and data on customer profiles.

http://www.bevinfogroup.com/ME2/default.asp

M. Shanken Communications, Inc.

Publishes *Impact* and *Market Watch*. These publications present data about wine consumption, market share, advertising expenditure and correlated information.

Publishes "The wine market in the United States: Analysis of the *Impact* data bank and forecasts," an exhaustive annual report which contains over 300 tables, charts and maps concerning the American wine market.

Publishes "The Global beverage market," an annual report from *Impact's* data bank about the situation of the alcoholic beverage sector in the world.

http://www.mshanken.com/

Practical Winery & Vineyard

A bi-monthly magazine with information and analyses on viticulture, winemaking and wine marketing.

http://www.practicalwinery.com/

The Gomberg-Fredrikson Report

Initially created by Louis Gomberg in the late 1940s, the Gomberg-Fredrikson Report is a unique source of information providing comparative tracking of monthly and annual shipments from California's main wineries and wine imports by country. This report also provides comments and discerning analysis of the current economic context and the trends that shape the market.

http://www.gfawine.com/

Vineyard & Winery Management

Publishes *Vineyard & Winery Management Magazine*, a bi-monthly professional magazine for vintners, vineyards and wineries from the East to West Coast, focusing on employee management, processes and technologies in the vineyards and the cellars.

Produces an annual publication, the "Wine industry Index" (formerly "Product Directory & Guide").

http://www.vwmmedia.com/

Wine Business Publications

Covering the commercial trends in its weekly *Wine Business Insider* newsletter and in the *Wine Business Monthly* review, which both target wine executives.

Also publishes the "Wine industry directory and almanac" every year.

http://www.winebusiness.com/

Wine Country Classifieds

Small ads for jobs and services in the alcoholic beverage industry.

Marketing Organic Wines in France

In France, many specialized magazines exist like the *Revue du Vin de France*, as well as many special wine supplements in daily newspapers (*Figaro Magazine, Le Monde, Les Echos, Le Point, L'Express*, etc.). These annual issues dedicated to wine prove the readers' interest in the subject. The many ads for estates and chateaux in these magazines reinforce this interest.

Eco-labels and Certification

Vintners produce organic wine according to specific regulations established by the certification agencies:

ECOCERT, created in 1991, is the most widespread and checks 70% of organic companies in France and 30% throughout the world. Ecocert certifies most organic wine.

AB is a label of the Agriculture Ministry and guarantees 95% of the ingredients as organic. The logo can be used on wine but is not systematically present. Many labels simply say "wine made with organically grown grapes" and are certified by Ecocert.

The **European organic logo** can also determine the organic nature of wines.

Other certifications such as "biodynamic" (Demeter, Biodyvin) or "Terra Vitis" promote sustainable agriculture. Convinced by the importance of HEV certification (High Environmental Value), the VIF (Vintners of France) have requested the creation of a logo promoting more environmentally sound agricultural practices.

French Consumers

French consumers understand what an organic product is but are still confused by organic wine labeling. However, according to *La Revue des Vins de France* (2011), organic wine has the reputation of the healthiest choice.

In essence, 83% of French participants had heard of organic wine, 53% through the media and 49% through in-store advertising. Of all participants, 39% said they had already bought organic wine and 17% said they regularly bought organic wine in supermarkets, directly from producers, from wine merchants or in specialized organic stores. On average, they paid 10.60 euros per bottle.

What is their general perception of organic wine? Even though it may be more expensive, it protects the environment and respects the wine producers.

Another study (2013) adds that those over 35 years of age and individuals with higher incomes are the key consumers of organic wine. It is a sincere approach to environmental discovery and exploration of new oenological territories. "L'art de vivre" (The art of living) is at the heart of the concerns of French people, as indicated by a recent survey by the magazine *Que Choisir* (October 2013) which shows that non-organic French wines have pesticide residues, in contrast to organic wines, which contain only a few.

Marketing Strategies of French Producers

To promote their wines, wineries use advertising campaigns, POS advertising, in-store promotions, hotels, restaurants, specialized stores, professional trade fairs and wine fairs. The organic sector in France is experiencing a resurgence of interest and even constitutes the *French touch*, according to many culinary experts. The great Chef Marc Veyrat (La Maison des Bois, near Annecy) expresses it like this: "The products of organic soil are a feature of French gastronomy, and I am very optimistic for the future, thanks to the development of organic and biodynamic agriculture." [14](*Journal Gault et Millau*, November 2013)

According to Thierry Duchenne from Sud Vin Bio (organizer of the Millésime Bio), wineries carry out private marketing studies to determine their strategy, which makes it difficult to obtain data. Among the 5,000 French producers, there are only a few large organic wineries; most are smaller estates with their own marketing strategies.

As a reference, a guide to the best French organic wines was published in 2010 (Gault et Millau).

The Example of Gilles Louvet Wines

Gilles Louvet is one of the largest French producers of organic wines and he sells on the American market.

Louvet was officially certified in 1993. Today he works in close collaboration with 50 producers and 10 wine cooperatives throughout France, and the size of his vineyards in Languedoc-Roussillon has practically quadrupled.

For his part, Louvet sees no difference between organic and non-organic wines: "Organic ingredients do not make the wine better or worse," he insists. "The vintner and the soil make the difference, not the production methods."[15]

Louvet exports seven of his "AB" labeled wines to the United States, which he sells to retailers and restaurants in Texas, Maine, Florida and North and South Carolina. He maintains offices in New York City. He has probably played a decisive role in the adoption of American and European regulations and the sub standardization of organic labels by conserving the organic label on his bottles in the very strict American organic market.

http://www.vignobles-gilleslouvet.com/

And Also...

In 2006, Château Fonroque became the first *grand cru* to obtain the French "AB" certification. The Romanée-Conti since 1985 has practiced organic farming in Burgundy.

Distribution

Supermarket chains and specialized stores are also responding to the growing demand. Thus, the brand of organic stores L'eau Vive (22.5 million euro turnover in 2012) currently has 31 stores and wishes to settle in cities of over 100,000 inhabitants. The brand is presently seeking to improve its cellar space, which currently offers 115 to 130 different wines. "We must recognize that profitability meter radius is not the best of our concept," explains its CEO, Didier Cotte. "We work not only on the offer to make it more consistent, but also the presentation for readability. 80% of our customers are indeed clients and they are not sensitive to merchandising by name."[16]

Wine fairs have been broadening their offer of organic wines over the last few years. For example, Monoprix offers over 34 references of "organic" or "biodynamic" wines (a list of organic Monoprix wines and their prices can be found in Appendix E). The customer profile (in general trendy city-dwellers looking for healthy products) can explain why they offer a greater selection of organic products.

The Price

According to an IPSOS 2013 consumer survey, **price is not an element that determines the purchase of organic wine**: only 30% of them mention this parameter for the purchase of organic wine, compared to 50% for the purchase of a non-organic wine. The number one criterion is respect for the environment, with the same importance as the wine's origin. On average, consumers buy organic wine for 14 euros when they are giving it as a gift, and spend 6.9 euros for their everyday wine; 35% had already purchased organic wine. The profile for these buyers corresponds to people who are very sensitive to the environment and organic food while also being wine connoisseurs.

The Positioning of French Wine

A 2010 UbiFrance study on organic wines on several key markets revealed different points of view.

In terms of the French organic wine market, the "AB" certification and label are recognized and considered trustworthy. They represent respect for the environment and a growing interest in organic products.

On the other hand, producing organic wine costs more, and certification does not guarantee quality, or may be used solely for marketing purposes. Furthermore, there is increasing international competition.

The Main Professional Trade Fairs and Organic Wine Fairs in France

- **Millésime Bio (Montpellier):** Every year in January, 700 international vintners present their wines to buyers from all over the world. The Millésime Bio Challenge is an international organic wine competition organized by the Trade Association of Organic Wines of Languedoc-Roussillon (Sudvinbio), created to help professionals and the general public recognize high quality organic wines.

- **Vivre Autrement Fair (Parc Floral, Vincennes):** Every year in March, with 400 exhibitors, including wine producers.

- **Eco-Bio Alsace Fair (Colmar):** May, with wine producers and conferences.

TABLE 26. Perspectives for French wines

Strengths	Weaknesses
• ORGANIC: differentiating factor • AB certification and logo are recognized • Respect for the environment: a flourishing theme	• Price: organic wines are more expensive than conventional wines • Certification does not guarantee a difference in quality • Progress to be made on winemaking standards • Lack of segmentation
Opportunities	**Risks**
• Growing interest of monopoly markets • Avenues to explore in the United States, Denmark, Italy • Growing consumer demand for organic produce	• Organic becomes the only selling point • Competition from Italian and New World wines (Australia, Chile)

Source: Ubifrance

- **Printemps Bio (throughout France):** For 2 weeks in June, organic market leaders promote their expertise to the general public. In June in Toulouse, the Agence Bio organizes the National Industry Forum.

- **Eco-Bio Fair:** Brittany in September.

- **Salon Marjolaine (Parc Floral, Paris):** November, with 550 exhibitors and 75,000 visitors, including organic wine producers.

- **Salon Asphodèle (Pau) December:** The largest organic wine fair in the Aquitaine region.

- **Organic Trade Fairs 2015/2016:** 6 towns in France promote everything organic, including wine:

  — Angers, Oct. 2015

  — La Rochelle, Apr. 2016

  — Le Mans, Apr. 2016

  — Poitiers, Nov. 2015

  — Rennes, Feb. 2016

  — Vannes, Jan. 2016

Notes

8   http://www.organicwinejournal.com/index.php/learn/

9   http://theorganicwinecompany.com/faqs/#q3

10   http://www.winespectator.com/blogs, Delmas, Study, Bren School of Environmental Science & Management, Santa Barbara, (2014)

11   http://www.frogsleap.com/the-story.php

12   http://www.campovida.com/posts/

13   Santa Cruz, California (PRWEB), June 28, 2012

14   Journal Gault et Millau, November 2013

15   http://www.vignobles-gilleslouvet.com/uk/actions_preserver_2.php

16   http://www.eau-vive.com/pa386/notre-histoire

Chapter 5
Organic Flavor and the Paradox of Consensus

The wine world is a world where taste is proof of quality. These new organic wines seem, despite the gratuitous but significant criticism, to incite unanimity, in every way. Paradoxically, organic wines are enabling the birth of a new world of wine, in an identical version of the food revolution of the last few years.

Organic Food: Another Alchemy
A Reputation Not Yet Established

Some criticize organic wine, tersely calling it undrinkable, vinegary or cheap-tasting. The polemic continues as certain public figures make random declarations, ensuring organic wine is the talk of the town and another point for consumer interest.

For wine professionals, advertisers or sommeliers, this reputation is outdated. Today, most organic wines are good. The return to a chemical balance in the wines has engendered a return to quality.

Nicolas de Rouyin expresses this idea ("Is organic wine better?" May 2012, http://bonvivantetplus.blogspot.com):

> *Is Organic viticulture better for the wine? An emeritus taster like Michel Bettane thinks it promotes depth in wine and reminds us that the quality of work in the cellar is essential to extract the best of it. Other taste professionals speak of a better expression of fruit, and some others say it is a way of improving the freshness of the wine.*[17]

This is echoed by Jean-Michel Deluc, former head sommelier at the Ritz: *"At one time, nine out of ten organic wines were bad,"* he remembers. *"But those were the early stages."*[18]

Antoine Gerbelle, Chief Editor of *Revue du Vin de France* and French wine critic, confirms certain criticisms about organic wines: *"The finish of many organic wines can be disappointing, can seem at little short."*[19]

Denis Durboudieu, who teaches oenology at Bordeaux University, believes, however, that all types of wines can taste bad. He adds, closing the debate:

> *We should be more surprised that there are still badly made wines: too much alcohol, tart, acidic, oxidized, fetid, sulfurous, lactic, rancid, phenolic, bitter, astringent, diluted, dried out, over-woody, leafy, moldy, earthy. These unforgivable faults unfortunately affect almost all wine categories: conventional, organic, natural, biodynamic. No standard could excuse these serious violations of wine and its goodness. Personally, all I ask is that the wine tastes good, makes me feel good, moves me. Its proclaimed persuasion is of no interest to me.*[20]

Finally, Jean-Robert Pitte, geographer and president of the Wine Academy of France, is expressing the same ideas: "The wine industry has evolved over the past decades and everyone agrees that the reduction of synthetic chemical inputs is a good thing. The ideal should be the general rule that the soil must be alive, fertilizers limited in amount and preferably natural, pesticides used as little as possible, and the natural yeast of the soil (both vineyard and cellar) be strong and abundant. But the best is the enemy of the good, and the fundamentalist rejection of any adjuvant treatment often leads to mediocre wines, even disasters. It is sometimes found, for example, in wines without sulfur. About biodynamics, practiced by some of the best winemakers in France and the world, it is likely to lead to great local wines but it is not an absolute guarantee of quality. We can't exclude rational vineyard management and winemaking. The only criterion is the enthusiastic verdict of the informed taster, and not a particular label on the bottle."[21]

A Different Chemistry

As you probably know, organic agriculture does not utilize chemical products such as fertilizers and pesticides. They are replaced by copper, represented mainly by the famous Bordeaux mixture. Biodynamics, faithful to Steiner's principles, adds two main preparations and many treatments as phyto-homeopathic dilutions. For their part, vintners making so-called "natural" wines leave the juice to its own devices during the wine's aging, banishing all or most sulfur during the different stages of wine making.

According to Antoine Gerbelle, it is a question of "make-up" which is not present in these natural wines: *"Flavored yeast and bludgeoning wood notes developed to stimulate and sweeten the length on the palate... Good organic vintners have no need for these artifices."*[22]

Despite the confusion generated by these different methods described in similar ways on labels, one of the consistencies in these three movements is a strong preference for the use of indigenous yeasts to ferment the musts, and renunciation of decades of research that helped create aseptic wines with developing aromas for a quick and surprise-free glass.

Basically, organic wine does not contain the same chemical components as conventional wine. Potassium sorbate is prohibited and the addition of sulfites is much regulated. It is limited at 100 mg per liter for red wine (versus 150 mg/l for conventional red) and 150 mg for white and rosé wines (versus 200 mg/l for conventional white and rosé).

These two chemical elements help stabilize the wine. Their absence makes it difficult to control: a second fermentation may occur in the bottle without potassium sorbate, while sulfur dioxide avoids microbial proliferation in the wine.

"If the grape has been well protected from cryptogamic and harmful disease, which is possible with organic but more difficult and more expensive with integrated or conventional agriculture, it will be just as good but not better. However, if the leaves were destroyed by mold or insects, if the grape rotted before ripening, it will not be possible to make good wine," adds Denis Dubourdieu, Professor of oenology at Bordeaux University and French winemaker.[23]

This is why organic wine can sometimes release a particular odor that is so heavily criticized. "There can be an unclean taste, an animal note of manure," notes Jean-Michel Deluc (former Head Sommelier at the Ritz, one of the world's best wine-tasters).

In the case of so-called natural wines, requirements are even more stringent as the addition of sulfites is very limited if not altogether prohibited. Tolerance stands at 30 mg/l for reds and 40 mg/l for whites.

"The absence of sulfites creates even worse deviances," assures Jean-Michel Deluc. *"We have found nothing better than sulfur to avoid bacteria. Without it, we are taking risks. In any case, these are not wines to lay down."*[24] Natural wines should therefore be drunk immediately.

This Demands Tremendous Expertise

What we learn from these enlightened analyses is that everything rests upon the expertise and know-how of the wine producers.

"Organic wine requires experience. It takes years to master organic wine," Jean-Michel Deluc recalls, citing great names who have succeeded in this delicate exercise: Domaine de Trévallon in Baux-de-Provence (Bouches-du-Rhône) (A leading French organic wine producer), or Huet in Vouvray (Indre-et-Loire), vintners who have been "in the organic system for twenty, thirty years."[25]

Organic winemaking can, however, derive a substantial advantage in terms of expertise. The vinification may be identical but the soil is completely different and its valorization even more important when it is worked organically.

Michel Véron, Professor of oenology at the Viticultural College of Champagne and author of an educational site and books, confirms,

For me, the quality of a wine is more associated with the expertise of the vintner than with the fact that the grapes are or are not organic. In Champagne, organic vintners that I know are passionate about what they do. They are aware of their impact on the environment and that is reflected in the vinification.[26]

This is in fact a vinicultural practice revisited through organic standards, or an exploration of artisan expertise enhanced by the organic industry. Producers create new bonds with the earth and their production, orienting their expertise differently and exploring new tastes. For these biodynamic producers with a genuine intellectual approach, a philosophical one as Goethe is considered the father of biodynamics (he wanted to understand the different kingdoms of nature and identify the rules of living; Steiner is considered one of his disciples), the practice goes beyond any idea of marketing or even looking for a taste of the beverage.

Michel Bettane and Thierry Desseauve, the French experts and ex-editors of "La revue du vin de France", leading French wine critics, explain their approach in a note published in January 2013 on the blog of Nicolas de Rouyn (http://bonvivantetplus.blogspot.com):

Biodynamic, according to the anthroposophist dogmas of Rudolf Steiner (1861–1925), an old-fashioned Australian philosopher whom agriculture ideas have been saved, refers to the belief that 'basically, humanity has to understand nature and living as a great whole and to undergo cycles related to astral configurations. Thus all bio-dynamic follow a calendar published by the great German priestess of the tribe, Maria Thun, which sets a good day to be involved in the preparations of the vine from plants, animals and minerals, mixed in basins of wood and copper to combat disease. Yet it would be foolish to deny the positive effects of viticulture which refers to these principles and that often leads to a considerable improvement in the biological life of the ground and therefore to the quality of the grapes, the flavor is more information from the carrier terroir. Immemorial knowledge has indeed realized the influence of cycles of the moon on the plant and any great physician knows that humanity also obeys biological cycles that make at times the effects of drugs and more effective treatments. But do not attribute the positive effects to the vine potions, silica buried in a cow's horn or stag's bladder. It is rather the result of intelligent homeopathic practices which involve a patient and scrupulous observation of the vine and tend to strengthen its natural defenses, improving its immune capabilities.[27]

A Taste of Terroir
New Winemaking Landscapes

This viticulture gives the terroir pride of place. Free of chemical excesses, it reconnects with the typicality of the soil, the weather, hydrology and plot orientations, even though some regions had moved away from that approach. Organic wines display a very particular taste, that of their terroir.

Nicolas de Rouyn described this phenomenon in his blog (http://bonvivant-etplus.blogspot.com, March 2011):

For more than twenty years after the first ecologists of the 1970s, awareness of the environment and a "clean" trend have emerged in the Vineyards. Hesitant at first, it became what experts call a trend...It is not only a very important to the public health movement, but also a return to the fields for a new generation. The desertification of the countryside is ending, a new generation returns to the earth.[28]

Organic vintners do not consider the nature of the terroir in the same way. For biodynamic growers it means an increasing use of local elements that were considered harmful in the past. So weeds are now called "self-propagating" and given pride of place. They allow soil maintenance and balance the vines' nourishment, even helping to fight disease through decoctions, with nettles for example.

The search for quality implies the maintenance and even the use of these plants and so the winemaking landscape is changing: embankments and hedges are conserved, and in turn the fauna is conserved, helping viticulture to become a precious ecological niche. Certain insects have been enlisted to help preserve the vines.

Paul Barre, from Château La Fleur Cailleau in Canon-Fronsac, conserves hedges, brambles and even uncultivated land.

Similarly, landscapes related to wine industry also change in connection with these sustainable trends. Forests, which produce barrels or wine stoppers, are also spaces for change. Jean-Charles Vicard (Vicard Tonnelleries) expresses this issue with me during a personal conversation:

"Representing the 6th generation of the coopering family Vicard is a rare and precious heritage. I undertake to work with my children so they will have all the weapons to be ready, if possible, to perpetuate this noble profession.

"Forest protection, and nature in general, is undoubtedly our battle, and we have to establish some connection with the bio/ecological culture. Respect for the different stages of forestry is our organic basis. Forestry is managed with rigor and passion by the National Office of Forests, and includes, in particular, cutting trees down during either waning or ascending moon.

"However, my involvement does not stop there… I am now convinced by the potential of oak tannins which would protect the wine with its anti-oxidant power, and which is a source of benefits to our health. So I really think we can do our best, dealing with Mother Nature with respect for the next generations."

A Return to Acidity and Floral Notes

Antoine Gerbelle affirms that there is a typical flavor to organic wines.

The well made organic red wines have an extra acidity which gives them a particular balance. Why? Because a vine that has never been given potash has a better acidity than a plant saturated with chemical fertilizer to increase its productivity. Unfortunately, most of the vines in France have been given far too much chemical fertilizer. When tasting red wines, I often notice with organic wines the presence of a floral expression that appears before the fruit. These floral notes are very rare in red wines made conventionally. Let's take the example of the Shiraz from Cornas, in the north of the Rhône Valley. When tasting these wines, connoisseurs often encounter very particular flavors, notes of soot and even tar. Well, when you taste Shiraz wines by Thierry Allemand, the reference in the area's organic wine, violet and iris dominate. Amazing floral purity! Finally, great organic wines often have slightly lower alcohol content than average. Combined with a higher acidity, this temperance helps create a better balance. We can see this with wines from 2003, the heatwave year when grand organic wines dazzled with their brilliance, like the Rasteau 2003 by Jérôme Bressy from Gourt de Mautens, or the Bourgueil Prestige from Stéphane Guion's Estate. Even as a primeur, this wine already revealed preserved fruit, extra acidity and more subtle aromas.

He continues with a specific example:

Clos Rougeard from the Foucault Brothers (...) is an exceptional Saumur-Champigny. Of course, here the freshness of the wine is first and foremost associated with a truly fabulous terroir. But the difference, thanks to organic viticulture, can be seen in the 'small' vintages. In this wine, there is no horrendous bouquet of green pepper, the plant aroma that marks most of the Cabernet Franc wines produced in the less successful years. But here, there is a genuine regularity because of the harmonious care of the vines. When you taste ten vintages, you're struck by the extraordinary consistency of the wine. This character comes directly from the grape, not the cellar-master. Every vine reproduces the shocks it has suffered (treatments, brutal pruning) over years and years.

Antoine Gerbelle irrevocably concludes,

When they are well made, organic wines express a tastier, more digestible maturity. It is like when you taste a nice piece of fruit from an old fruit tree. It is no riper than any of the others, but it has more presence on the palate, a presence that does not rely on sugar alone, but a balance of tastes. With a good organic white wine, for instance, you will notice immediately a peculiar volume in the mouth which is not built around alcohol. It is based on a density of flavor. I genuinely felt this when I was in Anjou, tasting wines by Richard Leroy, especially his cuvée Les Noëls de Montbenault, and the wines of Stéphane Bernaudeau, Les Nourrissons. These wines offered a truly unusual volume, never burning, never sweet, far from the one-dimensional profile of most dry white wines. You can sense the high quality of grapes from a plant whose growing cycle is slow and regular.[29]

Steven Spurrier is a British wine expert and former merchant in Paris, France, who has been described as a champion of French wine. Spurrier organized the Paris Wine Tasting of 1976 called "The judgment of Paris" which promoted the expansion of wine production in the new world.

I know little about the techniques of Bio-dynamism, but very much respect those estates who practice it, too many to mention. It is now agreed that quality of expression in wine comes from the vineyard, not the cellar. The vineyard therefore has to be farmed in the most honest, most natural way possible so that the vine's health and vigor can produce grapes that are as expressive as possible of the climate, the terroir and the varietal itself. Bio-dynamic viticulture allows the vines to flourish with natural energy to best achieve this. The motto of my school was 'A

Healthy Mind in a Healthy Body,' a simple, but not often achieved aim for a human being. For vines farmed bio-dynamically are trained to the same end.[30]

Proof of Quality
For Grand Crus

A large part of the greatest wines in the world are organic wines. In top position is the Domaine de la Romanée-Conti, whose Burgundy *grand crus* sell for thousands of euros. In a documentary shown in 2011 on France's France 3 TV channel, the estate's co-director Aubert de Villaine stated quite simply, "I can't see how a grand cru could be anything other than organic." [31]

So, Aubert de Villaine (and his co-director Henry-Frédéric Roch) were the first to warn Burgundy about weed killer and the asphyxia threatening the soils and endangering the terroir. The Romanée-Conti Estate has been using organic viticulture since 1986 and biodynamics since 2007.

This trailblazing estate produced six organic wines that won three stars for the first time, the highest distinction, in the 25th edition of the Hachette Wine Guide in 2010. These stars mean "an exceptional wine," and this guide is above any suspicion of partiality. It does not advocate a particular tradition, grape variety or winemaking method: "The wines are tasted blind, by industry professionals, who only assess their taste." Vincent Fleith, a vintner near Colmar whose Riesling Steinweig has won awards, refers to common sense, chance and science when explaining the taste of his wine.

Even if his family have been making wine for eleven generations, it was pure chance that he became specialized in organic wine. During his agricultural studies, he learned how to handle weed killers and fertilizers. But when he visited Australia and California, he realized that you can make wine differently, naturally. Vincent Fleith then progressively turned to organic viticulture, almost without knowing it, like Mr. Jourdain. "Initially, I didn't want anyone to know about it. I didn't mention it on the bottles—I thought that was too snobbish."

By stopping the use of fertilizers, he noticed that his wine slowly acquired a more decided taste. "The roots, which until then were lazing on the surface, must dig in the soil to find nourishment." He stopped killing the grass. "The roots compete with the grass, which we don't pull up anymore." Each plot develops its own characteristics from its own soil type, its own orientation. "Organic wine has more flavor than a conventional wine. The grapes own flavor is awakened."

Vincent Fleith is now perfecting his expertise. He chooses the plants to compost, and reduces copper inputs. "For my nine hectares, I barely use a kilo during the season, which is what I would have used previously for one spray session. I don't even need to chaptalize (add sugar), which my neighboring winemakers find hard to believe."[32]

TABLE 27. Some of the 18 organic wines that received 3 stars in the 2015 Hachette French Wine Guide:

Producer	Appellation	Cuvée
Chateau Barbarau	Clos Val Bruyère	2012
Domaine Fernand Engel	Gloekelberg Pinot gris	2012
Domaine de la Mordorée	Travel	2013
Domaine des Homs	Gravière de Sancastel	2012
Domaine Guilhem Barré	Sous le bois	2012
Marc Anstotz	Glintzberg Vielles Vignes	2012

TABLE 28. Organic European Wine List: Béatrice's recommendation (See American list Appendix E)

Producer	Appellation	Cuvée
Domaine Albert Mann	Alsace grand cru Furstentum pinot gris Le Tri, blanc	2011
Domaine Barmès-Buecher	Alsace grand cru Hengst cuvée François, blanc	2011
Domaine Bott-Geyl	Alsace grand cru Sonnenglanz gewurztraminer, Sélection de Grains Nobles, blanc	2007
Domaine Marc Tempé	Alsace grand cru Mambourg riesling, blanc	2008
Domaine Marcel Deiss	Alsace grand cru Altenberg de Bergheim, blanc	2011
Domaine Ostertag	Alsace Fronholz gewurztraminer Vendanges Tardives, blanc	2010
Domaine Valentin Zusslin	Alsace Bollenberg gewurztraminer Sélection de Grains Nobles, blanc	2009
Domaine Weinbach—Colette, Catherine et Laurence Faller	Alsace grand cru Mambourg gewurztraminer Vendanges Tardives, blanc	2010
Domaine Zind-Humbrecht	Alsace grand cru Rangen pinot gris, blanc	2011
Hugel et Fils	Alsace riesling Sélection de Grains Nobles, blanc	2011
Muré	Alsace grand cru Vorbourg Clos Saint-Landelin riesling, blanc	2010

Producer	Appellation	Cuvée
Château Guiraud	Sauternes	2011
Château Pontet-Canet	Pauillac	2011
Château des Rontets	Pouilly-Fuissé Les Birbettes, blanc	2010
Domaine d'Auvenay	Chevalier-montrachet grand cru	2011
Domaine de la Vougeraie	Musigny grand cru	2011
Domaine de Montille	Vosne-romanée premier cru Malconsorts cuvée Christiane, rouge	2011
Domaine des Comtes Lafon	Volnay premier cru Santenots du Milieu	2011
Domaine Drouhin-Vaudon	Chablis grand cru Les Clos	2011
Domaine du Comte Liger-Belair	La Romanée grand cru	2011
Domaine Jean Trapet Père et Fils	Chambertin grand cru	2011
Domaine Leroy	Musigny grand cru	2011
Domaine Rossignol-Trapet	Chambertin grand cru	2011
Domaine Vincent Dauvissat	Chablis grand cru Les Clos	2011
Joseph Drouhin	Vosne-romanée premier cru, Petits Monts	2011
Louis Latour	Chevalier-montrachet grand cru, Les Demoiselles	2011
Domaine Antoine Arena	Patrimonio, Carco, blanc	2011
Domaine André et MireilleTissot-Stéphane Tissot	Arbois, chardonnay Clos de La Tour de Curon	2010
Domaine Ganevat	Côtes du Jura, chardonnay Les Grands Teppes Vieilles Vignes 1919»	2011
Clos Marie	Coteaux du Languedoc—Pic Saint-Loup, Simon, rouge	2011
Domaine Peyre Rose	Coteaux du Languedoc, Clos des Cistes, rouge	2002
Mas Jullien	Coteaux du Languedoc, rouge	2010
Domaine Le Conte des Floris	Coteaux du Languedoc, Lune Blanche, blanc	2012
Château de Bellet	Bellet, rouge	2011
Clos Saint-Vincent	Bellet, Vino di Gio, rouge	2011
Domaine de Rancy	Rivesaltes, ambré	1973
Château Tirecul-La-Gravière	Monbazillac, Madame	2001
Domaine de la Cotelleraie	Saint-Nicolas-de-Bourgueil, L'Envolée	2010

Producer	Appellation	Cuvée
Domaine Huet	Vouvray, cuvée Constance	2003
Clos du Caillou	Châteauneuf-du-Pape, Les Quartz, rouge	2010
Domaine Giraud	Châteauneuf-du-Pape, Grenache de Pierre, rouge	2011
Domaine Les Bruyères-David Reynaud	Cornas, Le Rebelle	2011
M. Chapoutier	Ermitage L'Ermite, blanc	2011

And for Other Wines

"Whether they are occasional drinkers or faithful regulars of a type of wine, consumers are looking for healthy products with an authentic flavor. In this sense, organic wines are easy to drink, of good quality and broadly accessible. A reliable choice!", explains Pierre-Yves Blanchard, head wine buyer for the Naturalia stores.[33]

As Jean-Michel Deluc confirms, *"They are not laying down wines, but buying to lay down is a very French trait. In general, people don't keep their wines."* [34]

Good organic wines are clashing with AOC wines because they all claim the flavors of the terroir that are sought after today by consumers. These wines are, once again, criticized, and many columns have been written about organic wine in specialized magazines.

Consumers of organics are looking for surprises, and organic productions can satisfy this through vineyards that are still considered somewhat second-rate: California and its organic productions are becoming references in the wine world. Organic wines are increasingly promoted and mentioned, particularly in the *Wine Spectator* which interviewed Doug Bell, the wine buyer for Whole Foods, in November 2013. This chain of high-end grocery stores dedicates an increasing part of its wine purchasing to organic wines.

The French authority on the subject, Nicolas Joly, illustrates on the Domaine de la Coulée de Serrant website (http://coulee-de-serrant.com/fr/) the conviction and majestic expertise of biodynamic farming. By itself, Coulée de Serrant represents an *Appellation Contrôlée*. This vineyard was planted in 1130 by Cistercian monks and there have been vines there ever since. The estate was taken over by the Joly Family in 1961. It switched to biodynamics in 1981. A herd of cows produces the manure, a herd of sheep manage the grass between the vines in winter, and two hectares of the oldest vines are worked with horses.

Nicolas Joly is a pioneer, expert and amazing ambassador for biodynamics in France. As early as June 20, 2001, in the cellars of Château Smith Haut Lafitte at the time of the Vinexpo trade fair, Nicolas Joly was pleading for a more natural expression of French appellations: "An appellation is above all a soil associated with a micro-climate that the vine will incorporate in its grapes. To ensure that these singularities are fully expressed, the winemaker must make sure that each of his farming methods respects the surrounding natural life. The life of the soil first: exclusion of chemical weed killers and fertilizers. Life of the vine: exclusion of penetrative or systemic treatments that penetrate the sap and disturb photosynthesis, the source of flavor and aroma. When these methods are successful, the cellar work is much simpler." Most vintners who attended this event had already demonstrated their support for this code of ethics.[35]

For my part, the vineyards I manage have been practicing integrated agriculture since 1990 and I can only share my desire for increased yield without sacrificing quality over volume. I advocate viticulture that respects the land and does not impoverish the soil. A wine that safeguards taste quality and length in the mouth ("caudalies" were for a long time the sign of great quality) rather than favoring stock rotation and acceleration to increase cash flow.

Let's celebrate these thousands of years of progress in knowledge of the vine, the grapes and climates, centuries of expertise and innovations against disease. Let's use chemicals in moderation as we use medicines for our own health. Let's give priority to natural organic elements to preserve the balance of the earth and the vine.

Notes

17   "Is organic wine better?" May 2012, http://bonvivantetplus.blogspot.com

18   Guide des vins bio. M. Sargis, J.M. Deluc. Paru le 1 février 2006

19   http://www.larvf.com/,les-news-du-bio,13182.
     htm#xtor=cs1-5-[entree]-[10003]-[news_du_bio]-[menu_thematiques]

20   https://www.youtube.com/watch?v=v80p1QwGmjk

21   Histoire du paysage français: De la préhistoire à nos jours Broché —5 février 2003

22   http://www.larvf.com/,les-news-du-bio,13182.
     htm#xtor=cs1-5-[entree]-[10003]-[news_du_bio]

23   http://www.wine-searcher.com/m/2013/01/q-and-a-denis-dubourdieu-bordeaux.

24   Guide des vins bio. M. Sargis, J.M. Deluc. Paru le 1 février 2006

25   Guide des vins bio. M. Sargis, J.M. Deluc. Paru le 1 février 2006

26   http://www.guide-veron-champagne.fr/en/

27   http://bonvivantetplus.blogspot.com

28   http://bonvivantetplus.blogspot.com, March 2011

29   http://www.larvf.com/,les-news-du-bio

30   Academie Du Vin Guide to French Wines—May, 1992

31   http://www.bourgogne-live.com/2011/01/documentaire-exceptionne
      l-sur-france-3-une-camera-au-coeur-de-la-romanee-conti-pendant-quatre-saisons/

32   https://www.youtube.com/watch?v=QGN009g3Yuw

33   Le Figaro Vin, 13/11/2012 "Market shopping: the success of organic wines"

34   Guide des vins bio. M. Sargis, J.M. Deluc. Paru le 1 février 2006

35   http://www.wineanorak.com/biodynamic5.htm

Chapter 6

Investing in and Developing an Organic Vineyard: A Prospectus

There are many opportunities and difficulties around organic wine, which are summarized below. My recommendations are based on all the aspects necessary to successfully produce organic wine on today's market.

The Opportunities of Organic Wine

A Growing Market in the US and Most European Countries

- Health and environmental protection are rapidly expanding themes.
- There is a growing demand for high quality products.
- Consumers are more interested in green products.
- There is a growing demand for organic food and beverages in the United States and the European Union.
- Organic food sales have radically and regularly increased in the United States and in most European markets over the last ten years. Despite the recession, there is a long-term organic trend on the food market.
- Over the last few years, organic wines have increased in popularity similarly to other organic products.
- Wine's market penetration is increasing.
- Organic wine remains a niche wine market with development potential.

Increasing Numbers of Wine Producers are Adopting Sustainable Practices All Over the World

- Increasing numbers of wine producers in Europe and the United States choose to produce organic wine every year, including major wineries (see the increase in organic wine grape vineyard size).

- It is a "good deed" for the vineyard: environmental and health advantages of natural resource sustainability, increased resistance of the vines and adaptability to climate change. Emmanuel Cazes from Domaine Cazes in Roussillon, France notices "The soil became darker, acquired more humus content, and the acidity of the wine increased, the wines, quite simply, took on a fresher taste." [36] And Jean-Pierre Frick from Domaine Pierre Frick in Alsace, France adds, "The vines are more resistant and less vulnerable to grey rot and grape worm attacks. It is easier getting the grapes to ripen well." [37]

Organic Certification Can Provide Added Value on Certain Markets

- The USDA organic label is the most recognized eco-label on food and drink by American consumers.

- The "organic" (EcoCert) label is now highly recognized in Europe; it can work for American organic wine producers who export on the European market.

- Standardization of EU and US organic labeling is facilitating exports to Europe.

- Organic certification is a point of distinction in the highly competitive wine market.

- Organic certification is a means of adding value to environmentally sound practices.

- There is a new demand from stakeholders (sellers, media, consumers, regulators and environmental organizations) for credibility in the information provided by advertising and for transparency in farming practices. Organic certification can help meet this demand.

Improving Quality and Image

- According to a growing number of vintners, organic wine is of better quality and has better organoleptic characteristics.

- The media are focusing on organic wine, with increasingly positive reviews in the press.

- There are an increasing number of events and awareness campaigns which ensure the promotion of organic wine in the United States and Europe.

- The more "organic" labeled wines there are on the market, the more weight they will carry as established, recognized and appreciated products, which will help them become more popular.

- For growers, the ecological argument carries more weight than the financial argument:

  — Rémi Duchemin of Domaine Plan de l'Homme, Languedoc : "Today it's definitely a selling point, above all in the export market."[38]

  — Giovanni Menti, near Soave, agrees, "We're selling our wines more easily, especially for export, now that we're organic."[39]

  — Emmanuel Pageot of Domaine Turner-Pageot in Languedoc: "We want to be able to hand on a healthy winery to our children."[40]

  — Christine Saurel of Domaine Montirius in Rhône Valley concurs: "When you have children running about in the vineyard, you'd rather not spray the vines with toxic chemicals."[41]

Margins Can Be Maintained, Even with Higher Production Costs

- "Less competition than on the non-certified wine markets," at least on the American market, which suggests that there are still possibilities for growth and that margins can be greater.

- Organic consumers are ready to spend more for organic products.

- Specific characteristics of distribution channels: direct sales are greater than for conventional wines, which implies that there are fewer intermediaries and that the sales costs are lower.

The Difficulties of Organic Wine
Increased Competition

- Competition on the organic wine market is rapidly rising all over the world (see organic vineyards and vineyards in transition in Europe, the United States and also Australia, Chile, etc.).

- The number of organic wine brands significantly increases every year.

- In wine producing countries like the United States and France, organic wine consumption is almost entirely domestic, which means it is probably more difficult to export to these markets.

- Competition is strong throughout the wine market. At equal quality, organic wines are often less competitive than conventional wines because of their higher price.

Higher Production Costs Do Not Necessarily Mean Higher Prices

- The certification process, which can be complex and a little bureaucratic, means imposed costs.

- There are further costs when converting to organic practices.

- Labor costs are generally higher in an organic vineyard.

- "If there is a label on the wine, it creates a lesser image than that of traditional wines," which leads to lower prices for certain wines.

A Lasting Negative Perception in Terms of Quality

- Consumers' first experiences with sulfite-free organic wines were often negative and created preconceived ideas about organic wine.

- Wine can be considered a luxury product, for which quality is essential. Organic wine's reputation is lacking in terms of quality, which is a huge obstacle for consumer and buyer acceptance.

- Many wineries with good practices and even certification do not promote the organic aspect in the United States because of the negative perception of this label.

- The ban on sulfites can affect the quality, conservation and lifetime of the wine.

Consumer Confusion

- There are too many eco-labels in the United States; they are unclear for consumers, distributors, retailers and vintners.

- Excellent wines made with organic grapes are not labeled organic; consumers cannot therefore know the wine is organic.

- The "eco-laundering" of certain producers has added to the confusion and skepticism of consumers.

Lack of Marketing and Communication

- There are no international communication and marketing strategies for organic wine.

- Poor image: organic wine is not considered to be of better quality (on the contrary).

- There is a lack of consumer education; therefore they have little knowledge of organic wines and how they are produced.

- Supermarkets do not have clearly signed areas where consumers can buy organic wine. Organic products in wine stores are often displayed by grape variety or place of origin and mixed up with non-organic wines. Customers must ask for help in identifying the organic wines, which makes their buying experience less pleasant.

Sustainability is Not a Decisive Factor for Many Consumers

- Some consumers looking for wine take into account their own tastes, and not necessarily the greater good. Environmental certifications sometimes carry little weight.

- Some buyers are suffering from "eco-fatigue."

Recommendations

Considering all of this—the market trends, growth potential, and impact on the environment and consumer health—the benefits are worth the costs of investing in a sustainable vineyard.

However, the challenge of making a conventional winery sustainable is a huge commitment on many levels, with important financial and logistical considerations that must be carefully evaluated.

Following are some crucial considerations.

1. Considering USDA organic certification

   Of all the eco-labels around, there is one that sets itself apart, the USDA "organic" label, for the following reasons:

   — It is a certification with stringent standards and a respected logo (third party verification).

   — It is recognized on the American market and is a label that "counts."

   — There are fewer constraints than the "100% organic" label (5% of non-organic ingredients authorized), with a potential future relaxation of the regulations.

   — The USDA logo is authorized on the bottle.

   — It is a solid marketing tool.

   — It is internationally recognized if you are looking to export.

2. Choosing between two options to become organic

   When changing from a conventional vineyard to an organic one, the soils must be free of any chemical use for the past three years. There are two possibilities:

   — **Option 1:** Wait three years before growing organic vines and changing to organic wine.

   — **Option 2:** Buy organic grapes from another vineyard and change your equipment to machines designed for organic practices to get organic certification for the production procedures. This will mean you can sell organic wine while your vineyard is in its transition period.

3. Focusing first on the American market

   — The international wine market is growing in the United States, which is not the case in Europe.

   — The French organic wine market is a national market and export opportunities can be limited.

- The British market seems very competitive (because of the important role of supermarkets) and the organic food market has recently reduced in size.

- There may be export opportunities on the German market, either on the low-end or high-end markets, but with the cost of transport and taxes, export may not be competitive.

4. Investing in communications and marketing

- Marketing is a key element for educating consumers and buyers about organic wine production and how to recognize labels and logos.

- Communication is essential to give "green" wine a high quality image.

- Lobbying is required to harmonize eco-labels and their standards in the United States and to launch national communication campaigns about organic labels.

5. Implementing standards for wine

- **Quality:** Organic wine selections must be of a quality that is at least higher than average.

- **Extra price for organic:** Organic wine production implies costs that merit consideration. Grapes grown organically are sold on the free market at a higher price than conventionally grown grapes. Wine is a product that is judged according to its ingredients of "added value." Being made with organic grapes is a justified added value.

- **Value:** In the current economic context, these wines must be of reasonable value. Customers who buy these wines must believe that they are worth the price paid. They must also be within an everyday price range for consumers.

Notes

36   http://www.robertkacherselections.com/brand/maison-cazes#.VgmPXvlViko

37   http://returntoterroir.com/biodynamic-alsace-wine-pioneer-jean-pierre-frick/

38   http://www.wsj.com/articles/exports-of-french-wine-and-spirits-drop-sharply-1410272095

39   http://www.giovannimenti.com/?lang=en

40   http://www.turnerpageot.com/

41   http://www.montirius.com/notre-philosophie/

APPENDIXES

Appendix A
Certified Organic Wine Grape Producers—Members of the California Certified Organic Farmers (CCOF)

Producer	Chapter	Certified area (acres)	Certified products
A and A Agriculture	Fresno-Tulare	147	Grapes, grapes (wine)
Adastra Vineyards	North Coast	20	Grapes (wine)
Alary Vineyards	North Coast	12	Grapes (Chardonnay)
Alfaro Family Vineyards	Central Coast	8	Grapes (wine)
Alger Vineyards	North Valley	32	Grapes (wine)
Alma Rosa Vineyards & Winery	South Coast	7	Grapes (wine)
Amapola Creek Vineyards & Winery, Inc.	North Coast	36	Grapes (Cabernet Sauvignon), grapes (wine), wine
Annahala, LLC	Mendocino	206	Grapes (Pinot Noir)
Araujo Estate	North Coast	163	Grapes (wine), olive oil, olives, wine
Armstrong Vineyards	Big Valley	37	Grapes (Cabernet Sauvignon)
Arrowood Vineyards & Winery	North Coast	9	Grapes, grapes (Grenache), grapes (Merlot), grapes (Mourvèdre), grapes (Petit Verdot), grapes (Syrah), grapes (Viognier), olives, wine
Arroyo Seco Vineyards	Central Coast	572	Uncultivated land, grapes (wine)
Balinard Vineyard	North Coast	3	Uncultivated land, grapes (wine)

Producer	Chapter	Certified area (acres)	Certified products
Barbour-Wolf Vineyards	North Coast	8	Grapes (Cabernet Franc), grapes (Cabernet Sauvignon), grapes (Petit Verdot), grapes (Sauvignon Blanc), grapes (wine)
Barham-Mendelsohn Vineyard	North Coast	5	Grapes (wine)
Bartolucci Vineyards	Mendocino	166	Grapes (Cabernet Sauvignon), grapes (Chardonnay), grapes (Merlot), grapes (Muscat), grapes (Petite Syrah), grapes (Sauvignon Blanc), grapes (Syrah)
Beaver Creek Vineyards	Mendocino	39	Barley, uncultivated land, grape juice, grapes (Cabernet Franc), grapes (Cabernet Sauvignon), grapes (Petite Syrah), grapes (Sauvignon Blanc), hops, olive oil, vegetables, walnuts, vine, vinification
Beckstoffer Vineyards	Mendocino	50	Uncultivated land, grapes (Chardonnay), grapes (wine)
Bednar Vineyard	Mendocino	4	Grapes (Carignan), grapes (Syrah)
Benziger Family Winery	North Coast	5	Grapes (wine), wine
Bertagna Orchards, Inc.	North Valley	151	Almonds, grapes (Petite Syrah), grapes (Sangiovese), grapes (vin), blanching, packaging, hulling, sorting, wine
Bevill Vineyard Mgmt LLC	North Coast	11	Grapes (Cabernet Sauvignon), olives
Big Basin Vineyards	Central Coast	10	Grapes (wine), olives
Bill & Dan Prosperi	Fresno-Tulare	27	Grapes (Cabernet Sauvignon), grapes (Sauvignon Blanc)

Producer	Chapter	Certified area (acres)	Certified products
Bokisch Vineyards	Big Valley	84	Grapes, grapes (Chardonnay), grapes (Grenache), grapes (Merlot), grapes (Syrah), grapes (Viognier), grapes (wine)
Boudreaux Vineyards, LLC	North Coast	6	Grapes (Chardonnay), grapes (Pinot Noir), olives
Boulder Ridge	San Luis Obispo	22	Avocados, pineapple guavas, grapes (Pinot Noir), grapes (Syrah)
BR Cohn Vineyards and Winery	North Coast	8	Grapes (wine)
Brennan Vineyards	Mendocino	5	Grapes (Zinfandel)
Brereton Family Vineyard	North Coast	13	Grapes (Cabernet Sauvignon)
Burgess Yountville	North Coast	50	Grapes (Cabernet Sauvignon), grapes (Grenache), grapes (Merlot), grapes (Petit Verdot), grapes (Syrah), grapes (wine)
Caballo Blanco Vineyards	Mendocino	14	Grapes (Carignan), grapes (Petite Syrah), grapes (Zinfandel)
Calera Vineyard	Central Coast	83	Grapes (wine)
Canihan Vineyards	North Coast	15	Grapes (wine)
Carpenter Orchard Inc.	Mendocino	78	Grapes (Sauvignon Blanc), grapes (wine), pears, nuts
Cat's Paw Vineyards	Mendocino	8	Grapes (Merlot)
Chance Creek vineyard	Central Coast	18	Uncultivated land, grapes (Sangiovese), grapes (Sauvignon Blanc), grapes (Viognier), wine
Chappellet vineyard	North Coast	97	Grapes (Cabernet Sauvignon), grapes (Petit Verdot), grapes (wine)
Charmar Vineyards	North Coast	3	Grapes (Merlot)

Producer	Chapter	Certified area (acres)	Certified products
Chase Vineyards	Mendocino	46	Grapes (Carignan), grapes (Petite Syrah), grapes (Zinfandel)
Chavez & Leeds Vineyards	North Coast	35	Grapes (wine), olives
Clif Family Farm	North Coast	11	Uncultivated land, fruit and vegetables, olives, vine (grapes)
Cline Organic	North Valley	4	Uncultivated land, grapes (wine)
Clockspring Vineyards	Sierra Gold	350	Grapes (wine)
Coates/Coates Organic Vineyards	Humboldt-Trinity	22	Almonds, apricots, broccoli, cantaloupe melons, carrots, cauliflower, cherries, chestnuts, cucumber, figs, hazelnuts, flowers, garlic, grapes (Cabernet Sauvignon), grapes (Merlot), grapes (Petite Syrah), grapes (Sangiovese), grapes (Syrah), grapes (wine), grapes (Zinfandel), kiwis, lettuces, olives, onions, peaches, peas, peppers, plums, potatoes, spinach, tomatoes (cherry), tomatoes (heirloom), watermelons, wine.
Cold Creek	Mendocino	10	Grapes (Gewurztraminer), grapes (wine)
Cooper-Garrod Estate Vineyards	Central Coast	28	Grapes (Cabernet Franc), grapes (Cabernet Sauvignon), grapes (Chardonnay), grapes (Merlot), grapes (Pinot Noir), grapes (Syrah), grapes (Viognier), grapes (wine), wine, vinification

Producer	Chapter	Certified area (acres)	Certified products
Cox Vineyards	Mendocino	292	Uncultivated land, grapes (Cabernet Sauvignon), grapes (Carignan), grapes (Chardonnay), grapes (Merlot), grapes (Petite Syrah), grapes (Sauvignon Blanc), grapes (wine), grapes (Zinfandel)
Crazy Flower Vineyards	North Coast	4	Grapes (Cabernet Franc), grapes (Merlot)
Dalla Gasperina Vineyard	North Coast	15	Grapes (Cabernet Sauvignon), grapes (Petit Verdot), grapes (Sauvignon Blanc), grapes (Sémillon)
Damiano Vineyards	Mendocino	6	Grapes (Merlot)
Dana Estates Inc.	North Coast	58	Grapes (Cabernet Sauvignon), grapes (wine), olives
Daniel Vesely	Pacific Southwest	19	Apples, apricots, avocados, blackberries, cherries, redcurrants, figs, grapes (wine), vegetables, nectarines, olives, peaches, pears, persimmons, plums, pomegranates, stoned fruit, vegetables, walnuts
Davis Drive Organic	Mendocino	46	Grapes (Chardonnay), grapes (Muscat), grapes (Viognier)
De Coninck Vineyards	North Coast	149	Grapes, grapes (Cabernet Franc), grapes (Cabernet Sauvignon), grapes (Chardonnay), grapes (Merlot), grapes (Petit Verdot), grapes (Sauvignon Blanc)
Del Rio Vineyard	North Coast	20	Grapes (wine)
Deloach Vineyards	North Coast	17	Grapes (Chardonnay), grapes (Pinot Noir), fruit and vegetables

Producer	Chapter	Certified area (acres)	Certified products
Dever Family Vineyard	North Coast	4	Grapes (Cabernet Sauvignon)
Devoto Vineyards, LLC	Mendocino	116	Grapes (Merlot), grapes (Sauvignon Blanc), grapes (Viognier), grapes (wine)
Dierke Enterprises	North Coast	36	Apples, grapes (Pinot Noir), grapes (wine), hay and pasture, vegetables
Carneros Estate Winery	North Coast	316	Grapes (Chardonnay), grapes (Pinot Noir), wine and sparkling wine
Donald Lucchesi	Mendocino	16	Grapes (Carignan), grapes (Merlot)
Edge Hill	North Coast	6	Grapes, grapes (Carignan), grapes (Grenache), grapes (Mourvèdre), grapes (Petite Syrah), grapes (Zinfandel)
Elk Mountain Vineyards	Mendocino	26	Grapes (Sauvignon Blanc), grapes (wine), walnuts
Elkfield Vineyards	Mendocino	48	Grapes (wine)
Embros Vineyard	Mendocino	9	Grapes (wine), wine
Emilio's Terrace Vineyard	North Coast	7	Uncultivated land, grapes (wine)
Emtu Estate Wines/ Labyrinth Vineyards	North Coast	3	Grapes (wine)
Enterprise Vineyards	North Coast	192	Uncultivated land, fruit, grapes, grapes (Cabernet Franc), grapes (Cabernet Sauvignon), grapes (Grenache), grapes (Marsanne), grapes (Merlot), grapes (Mourvèdre), grapes (Petite Syrah), grapes (Petit Verdot), grapes (Roussanne), grapes (Sangiovese), grapes (Sauvignon Blanc), grapes (Syrah), grapes (Viognier), grapes (wine)...

Producer	Chapter	Certified area (acres)	Certified products
Enterprise Vineyards (continued)	North Coast	192	... grapes (Zinfandel), vegetables, olive oil, olives, pomegranates
Estines Vineyards	North Coast	3	Grapes (Pinot Noir)
Estrella River	San Luis Obispo	67	Grapes (wine)
Vins Et Al., Inc.	Central Coast	25	Grapes (Cabernet Sauvignon)
Fasi Estate Vineyard	Fresno-Tulare	42	Grapes (wine), wine
Favia Erickson Vintners	North Coast	1	Chamomile, fruit and nut trees, grapes (Sauvignon Blanc), grapes (wine), vegetables
Feingold Vineyards	North Coast	9	Grapes (wine)
Fetzer Vineyards	Mendocino	1841	Cherries, uncultivated land, grapes, grapes (Cabernet Franc), grapes (Cabernet Sauvignon), grapes (Chardonnay), grapes (Grenache), grapes (Merlot), grapes (Mourvèdre), grapes (Muscat), grapes (Nebbiolo), grapes (Petite Syrah), grapes (Petit Verdot), grapes (Pinot Noir), grapes (Roussanne), grapes (Sangiovese), grapes (Sauvignon Blanc), grapes (Syrah), grapes (Viognier), grapes (Zinfandel), lavender, olives
Flook Farms and Vineyards	Mendocino	60	Grape (Syrah), walnuts
Flora Bella Farm	Fresno-Tulare	20	Dried apricots, dried nuts and fruit, fruit, grapes (wine), vegetables, tomatoes (dried)

Producer	Chapter	Certified area (acres)	Certified products
Foote Path Farm	Pacific Southwest	20	Figs, grapefruit, grapes (wine), lemons, limes, pomegranates, quinces, tangelos, tangerines
Forenzo Vineyards	Mendocino	7	Grapes (wine)
Four Gates Vineyard	Central Coast	4	Grapes (wine)
Frog's Leap Winery	North Coast	155	Laying hens, eggs, fruit, grapes (wine), fruit and vegetables, vegetables, olives, ornamental plants, orchard fruit
Galleano Enterprises, Inc.	Pacific Southwest	375	Grapes (wine), grapes (Zinfandel)
Gamble Vineyard	North Coast	26	Grapes (Cabernet Sauvignon), grapes (Sauvignon Blanc), grapes (Sémillon)
Gasto Farms	Fresno-Tulare	75	Grapes (Colombard)
Giberti Vineyards	North Coast	1	Grapes (Pinot Noir)
Gibson Farm	Mendocino	16	Grapes (Merlot), grapes (Sangiovese)
Goforth Vineyards	Mendocino	6	Grapes (Petite Syrah), grapes (Zinfandel)
Graziano Vineyards	Mendocino	21	Grapes (wine)
Grebennikoff Vineyards	North Coast	5	Grapes (wine)
Green Valley Vineyards, Inc.	North Coast	5	Grapes (wine)
Grider Home farm	Mendocino	27	Grapes, grapes (Cabernet Sauvignon), grapes (Chardonnay), grapes (Merlot), grapes (Zinfandel)
Guru Ram Das Orchards	Yolo	17	Almonds, apricots, citrus fruit, dried fruit, grapes (wine), peaches, persimmons, plums, walnuts
Gusto Vineyards	Mendocino	10	Uncultivated land, grapes (Carignan), grapes (Petite Syrah), grapes (wine)

Producer	Chapter	Certified area (acres)	Certified products
Haiku Vineyard, LLC	Mendocino	165	Grapes (Chardonnay), grapes (Sauvignon Blanc), grapes (Syrah), wine
Haire Management Company LLC	North Coast	29	Grapes (Pinot Noir)
Hall Wines	North Coast	283	Grapes (Cabernet Franc), grapes (Cabernet Sauvignon), grapes (wine)
Hambrecht Vineyards	North Coast	74	Grapes, grapes (wine)
Handley Cellars	Mendocino	29	Grapes (Chardonnay), grapes (Gewurztraminer), grapes (Pinot Noir)
Hank & Linda Wetzel	North Coast	8	Grapes (Cabernet Sauvignon)
Happy Valley Farm	Central Coast	53	Apples, grapes (wine), pears
Harris Napa Valley Farm, LLC	North Coast	29	Grapes, grapes (wine), olive oil, olives
Harrison Vineyards	Mendocino	8	Grapes (wine)
Hartford Wood Road	North Coast	8	Grapes (Zinfandel)
Hartje Vineyards	Mendocino	10	Grapes (Grenache), grapes (Syrah)
Hawley Vineyards	North Coast	9	Grapes (Cabernet Franc), grapes (Cabernet Sauvignon), grapes (Merlot), grapes (Petite Syrah), grapes (Viognier), grapes (Zinfandel), wine
Heibel Ranch Vineyards	North Coast	2	Grapes (Cabernet Sauvignon), grapes (Petite Syrah), grapes (Zinfandel)
Hill Creek Farm	Mendocino	5	Grapes (Sauvignon Blanc), olives
Hillside Vineyards	Mendocino	40	Grapes (Sauvignon Blanc), grapes (Zinfandel)
Hoover Vineyards	Mendocino	6	Grapes (Carignan), grapes (Zinfandel)
Inglenook	North Coast	154	Grapes (wine)

Producer	Chapter	Certified area (acres)	Certified products
Inland Farm	Mendocino	13	Grapes (Cabernet Sauvignon), grapes (Chenin Blanc), grapes (Colombard), vegetables
Jack Neal & Son, Inc./ Dyson Smith	North Coast	4	Grapes (wine)
Jack Neal & Son, Inc./ Franklin	North Coast	6	Grapes (wine)
Jack Neal & Son, Inc./ Heitz	North Coast	105	Grapes (wine), olives
Jack Neal & Son, Inc./Heitz Ink Grade vineyard	North Coast	99	Grapes (Sauvignon Blanc), grapes (wine)
Jack Neal & Son, Inc./ Heitz Winery	North Coast	33	Grapes (wine)
Jack Neal & Son, Inc./ Heitz Zinfandel Lane Vineyards	North Coast	16	Grapes (wine)
Jack Neal & Son, Inc./ Martha's North, South & West	North Coast	33	Grapes (wine)
Jack Neal & Son, Inc./ Neal 1, 2, 3	North Coast	18	Grapes (wine), olive oil, olives
Jack Neal & Son, Inc./ Pelosi River Run	North Coast	7	Grapes (wine)
Jack Neal & Son, Inc./ Rutherford Farm	North Coast	9	Grapes (wine)
Jack Neal & Son, Inc./ Ackerman Vineyards	North Coast	10	Grapes (wine)
Jack Neal & Son, Inc./ Dutch Henry	North Coast	2	Grapes (wine), olives
Jack Neal & Son, Inc./ La Fata	North Coast	1	Grapes (wine), olive oil, olives
Jack Neal & Son, Inc./ Lacob Vineyards	North Coast	19	Grapes (wine), olives
Jack Neal & Son, Inc./ McCarthy	North Coast	8	Grapes (wine)
Jack Neal & Son, Inc./ Tucker Vineyards	North Coast	4	Grapes (wine)

Producer	Chapter	Certified area (acres)	Certified products
Jack Neal & Son, Inc./ Williams Vineyards	North Coast	2	Grapes (wine)
Jackson Family Wines	North Coast	59	Grapes (Cabernet Franc), grapes (Merlot)
JCP Farm	Mendocino	22	Grapes (Cabernet Sauvignon), grapes (Sauvignon Blanc), grapes (Zinfandel)
Joe Galleano	Fresno-Tulare	108	Grapes (Cabernet Sauvignon), grapes (Centurion), grapes (Grenache), grapes (Merlot), grapes (Pinot Noir), grapes (Ruby Cabernet), grapes (Riesling Blanc)
Joe Soghomonian, Inc.	Fresno-Tulare	582	Almonds, redcurrants, grapes, grapes (Carignan), grapes (Colombard), grapes (Grenache), grapes (raisins), grapes (table), raisins, walnuts
Johnson Orchards & Vineyards, Inc.	Mendocino	14	Apples, grapes (Carignan), grapes (Zinfandel), walnuts
Johnston Vineyards	North Coast	6	Grapes (wine)
Juliana Vineyards	North Coast	8	Grapes (Cabernet Sauvignon)
Kathryn Kennedy Winery	Central Coast	7	Grapes, grapes (Cabernet Sauvignon), wine
Kimsey Vineyard	South Coast	23	Grapes (wine)
Kivelstadt Vineyards	North Coast	10	Grapes (Pinot Noir), grapes (Syrah), grapes (Viognier)
Komes Farm, LLC	North Coast	119	Grapes, grapes (Cabernet Franc), grapes (Cabernet Sauvignon), grapes (Merlot)
La Encantada Vineyard	South Coast	97	Grapes (Chardonnay), grapes (Pinot Noir), grapes (wine)

Producer	Chapter	Certified area (acres)	Certified products
La Ribera Vineyards	Mendocino	139	Uncultivated land, grapes (Chardonnay), grapes (Sauvignon Blanc), grapes (Syrah), grapes (wine), grapes (Zinfandel)
Lake Mendocino Vineyards	Mendocino	3	Grapes (Syrah), grapes (Zinfandel)
Lamanuzzi and Pantaleo	Fresno-Tulare	122	Grapes, grapes (Cabernet Sauvignon), grapes (Chardonnay), grapes (Mourvèdre), grapes (Nebbiolo), grapes (Sauvignon Blanc), grapes (wine)
LaRocca Vineyards	North Valley	162	Uncultivated land, grapes (wine), wine, wine bottling, winemaking
Larry Hirahara Family Farm	Fresno-Tulare	75	Blueberries, uncultivated land, grapes, grapes (Carignan)
Lauren Beuving	Mendocino	1	Grapes (Chardonnay)
Lavender Ridge Vineyard, Inc.	Sierra Gold	8	Grapes (wine), lavender, olives, wine
Leonardis Organic	Mendocino	387	Flowers, fruit, grapes (wine), fruit and vegetables vegetables, walnuts
Light Vineyards	Mendocino	23	Grapes (wine)
De Lisa Vineyard	North Coast	12	Grapes (wine)
Lockewood Acres	Yolo	8	Almonds, peaches, apricots, artichokes, Asian pear, asparagus, avocados, basil, beetroot, blackberries, blueberries, cabbages, broccoli, cantaloupe melons, chard, cherries, chives, eggplant, figs, garlic, gourds, grapefruit, grapes (raisins), grapes (wine), guava, hay, garden herbs, honey, jujube, kiwis...

Producer	Chapter	Certified area (acres)	Certified products
Lockewood Acres (continued)	Yolo	8	... lemons, lettuces, limes, mandarins, various leafy vegetables, nectarines, olives, onions, oranges, passion fruit, peaches, peppers, persimmons, pistachios, plums, pluots, pomegranates, potatoes, pumpkins, raspberries, rhubarb, rye, salad mix, squashes, strawberries, sweetcorn, tangelos, tangerines, tomatillos, tomatoes, watermelons, wheat
Lolonis Family Vineyards and Winery, Inc.	Mendocino	109	Grapes, grapes (Cabernet Sauvignon), grapes (Carignan), grapes (Chardonnay), grapes (Merlot), grapes (Sauvignon Blanc), grapes (Sémillon), grapes (Zinfandel)
Long Meadow Farm	North Coast	75	Grapes, grapes (Cabernet Sauvignon), grapes (Merlot), grapes (Sangiovese), grapes (Sauvignon Blanc), olives
Lorenzi Vineyards	Mendocino	28	Grapes (Cabernet Sauvignon), grapes (Merlot), grapes (Zinfandel)
Luna Matta Vineyards	San Luis Obispo	84	Grapes (wine), olives, walnut
Maboroshi Vineyards & Estates LLC	North Coast	12	Grapes (Pinot Noir)
Madonna Vineyards	North Coast	159	Uncultivated land, grapes (wine)
Magnificat Endeavors	Pacific Southwest	20	Avocados, grapes (wine), oranges (Valencia), tangelos

Producer	Chapter	Certified area (acres)	Certified products
Makela Olive Co.	South Coast	101	Uncultivated land, grapes (Chardonnay), garden herbs, lemons, olive oil, olives, packaging, vegetables
Marimar Estate	North Coast	60	Grapes (wine)
Martorana Family Vineyard, LLC	North Coast	30	Grapes (Cabernet Sauvignon), grapes (Chardonnay), grapes (Merlot), grapes (Petite Syrah), grapes (Zinfandel)
McClone Farm	Sierra Gold	17	Apples, grapes (wine), pears
McEvoy of Marin, LLC	North Coast	118	Blueberries, flowers, fruit, grapes, grapes (wine), garden herbs, jam, mushrooms, olive oil, processing olives into olive oil, olives, ornamental plants, transplanting, vegetables, wild herbs
McFadden Farm	Mendocino	512	Basil, bay leaves, beef, cattle (slaughtering), chili peppers, plant cover, garlic powder, grapes (Chardonnay), grapes (Sauvignon Blanc), grapes (wine), handling, garden herbs, lemon thyme, marjoram, onion flakes, oregano, pasture, prairies, rosemary, sage, mixed spices, savory, tarragon, thyme, wine
Medlock Ames Vintners, LLC	North Coast	316	Uncultivated land, grapes (wine), fruit and vegetables, olives
Mettler Family Vineyards	Big Valley	72	Grapes (Cabernet Sauvignon), grapes (Petite Syrah), grapes (Zinfandel)

Producer	Chapter	Certified area (acres)	Certified products
Milani Vineyards	Mendocino	68	Grapes (Cabernet Sauvignon), grapes (Chardonnay), grapes (Petite Syrah), grapes (Zinfandel)
Miralago Vineyard	Mendocino	5	Grapes (wine)
Molinari Vineyards	North Coast	11	Grapes (wine)
Morrison Vineyard	North Coast	4	Grapes (wine)
Murphy Creek Vineyards	Big Valley	58	Fruit, goats (last third of the gestation period), grapes (Cabernet Sauvignon), pasture & prairies, ewes (last third of the gestation period)
Murray Farm	North Coast	50	Apples, grapes (wine), lavender
Navone Vineyards	North Coast	27	Grapes (Cabernet Sauvignon), grapes (wine)
NBV	Mendocino	5	Grapes (Pinot Noir), wine
Neal Family Vineyards	North Coast	15	Grapes (Cabernet Sauvignon), olive oil, olives, wine
Neese Vineyards	Mendocino	107	Uncultivated land, grapes (Cabernet Sauvignon), grapes (Chardonnay), grapes (Merlot), grapes (Zinfandel)
Nelson Family Vineyards	Mendocino	17	Grapes (Muscat), grapes (Viognier), grapes (wine)
Neyers Farm	North Coast	13	Grapes (wine)
Nick J. Nazaroff	Fresno-Tulare	59	Grapes (Merlot), grapes (raisins)
Nova Vineyards	Mendocino	36	Grapes (Zinfandel)
Oak Pointe Farms	Kern	50	Uncultivated land, grapes (wine)

Producer	Chapter	Certified area (acres)	Certified products
Oakville Ranch Vineyards LLC	North Coast	68	Uncultivated land, grapes, grapes (Cabernet Franc), grapes (Cabernet Sauvignon), grapes (Chardonnay), grapes (Petite Syrah), grapes (Petit Verdot), grapes (Zinfandel)
Omnia Terra, LLC	North Coast	18	Apples, grapes (Cabernet Franc), grapes (Cabernet Sauvignon), grapes (Merlot), grapes (Petit Verdot), grapes (Syrah), nectarines, peaches, pears, plums
Pacific International Marketing (PIM)	Central Coast	564	Artichokes, arugula, beans (fresh), beetroot, bell peppers, bok choi, broccoli, cabbage, carrot, cauliflower, celeriac, celery, chard, coriander, cavolo nero, corn (fresh), dill, endive, escarole, uncultivated land, fennel, frisée, grapes (wine), shallots, iceberg lettuce, green cabbage, kohlrabi, lavender, leafy vegetables, leeks, lettuces, mustard leaves, olive oil, olives, onions, parsley, chili peppers, radishes, romaine, hearts of romaine, mixed herbs, spinach, spring mix, strawberries, tomatoes (fresh), turnip tops, watermelons.
Page's Bio	Pacific Southwest	4	Citrus, grapes (wine), fruit and vegetables, transplanting
Palo Alto Vineyard Management, LLC	North Coast	38	Grapes (wine)
Papa's Perch	North Coast	1	Grapes (wine)

Producer	Chapter	Certified area (acres)	Certified products
Parducci Vineyards	Mendocino	93	Grapes, grapes (Cabernet Sauvignon), grapes (Grenache), grapes (Petit Verdot), grapes (Syrah), grapes (Zinfandel)
Bio Patianna Vineyards, LLC	Mendocino	75	Grapes (Chardonnay), grapes (Sauvignon Blanc), wine
Peju Province Winery Ltd	North Coast	22	Grapes (wine)
Pierce Family Farm	Humboldt-Trinity	53	Carrots, plant cover, cucumber, uncultivated land, flowers, garlic, ginseng, grapes, grapes (wine), kiwis, melons, vegetables, onions, peaches, peppers, tomatoes (fresh)
Ponderosa Vineyards	Sierra Gold	36	Grapes (wine), pasture, grapes (wine)
Portola Vineyards, LLC	Central Coast	2	Grapes (wine)
Rancho Bernat	South Coast	4	Grapes (Cabernet Sauvignon), grapes (Nebbiolo), grapes (Sangiovese), wine
Ravenswood Estate Vineyards	North Coast	14	Grapes (Grenache), grapes (Merlot), grapes (Petite Syrah), grapes (wine), grapes (Zinfandel)
RB Wine Associates	Mendocino	29	Grape juice, grapes (Cabernet Sauvignon), grapes (Syrah), wine, wine (sparkling), winemaking
Redwood Valley Juice Production Company	Mendocino	2	Grapes (Carignan), grapes (Grenache)

Producer	Chapter	Certified area (acres)	Certified products
Redwood Valley/Barra of Mendocino/Girasole Vineyards	Mendocino	220	Uncultivated land, grapes (Cabernet Sauvignon), grapes (Chardonnay), grapes (Merlot), grapes (Muscat), grapes (Petite Syrah), grapes (Petit Verdot), grapes (Pinot Noir), grapes (Sangiovese), grapes (Syrah), grapes (wine), grapes (Zinfandel), olives, wine
Retzlaff Vineyards	Central Coast	11	Grapes (wine)
Ricetti Vineyards	Mendocino	114	Apples, figs, grapes (Carignan), grapes (Chardonnay), grapes (Colombard), grapes (Merlot), grapes (Petite Syrah), grapes (wine), grapes (Zinfandel), plums, vegetables
Robert Bollens & Cynthia Bollens	Mendocino	4	Grapes (Cabernet Sauvignon)
Robert Sinskey Vineyards	North Coast	175	Fruit, grapes (wine), olives
Rosewood Vineyards	Mendocino	41	Uncultivated land, grapes (Cabernet Sauvignon), grapes (Carignan), grapes (Merlot), grapes (Mourvèdre), grapes (Petite Syrah), grapes (Zinfandel)
Rustling Ridge Vineyards	North Coast	2	Grapes (Pinot Noir), olives
S. W. Emmert	Fresno-Tulare	40	Grapes (Ruby Cabernet)
Samuel Brannan Vineyards	North Coast	23	Grapes (wine)
Sangiacomo Family Vineyards	North Coast	23	Grapes (Chardonnay)

Producer	Chapter	Certified area (acres)	Certified products
Saracina Vineyards	Mendocino	55	Grapes (Cabernet Sauvignon), grapes (Chardonnay), grapes (Petite Syrah), grapes (Roussanne), grapes (Sangiovese), grapes (Sauvignon Blanc), grapes (Riesling Blanc), grapes (wine), grapes (Zinfandel), olive oil, olives, wine, winemaking
Scaggs Vineyard	North Coast	3	Fruit and nut trees, grapes (Grenache), grapes (Mourvèdre), grapes (Roussanne), grapes (Syrah), olives, walnuts, wine
Sciacca Vineyards	Mendocino	3	Grapes (wine)
Sentinel Hill Vineyards, LLC	Central Coast	20	Grapes (Cabernet Franc), grapes (Merlot)
Shayneh Vista Vineyards	North Coast	1	Grapes (wine)
Silver Mountain Vineyards	Central Coast	18	Grapes (Chardonnay), grapes (Pinot Noir)
Skipstone Farm	North Coast	39	Grapes (wine), fruit and vegetable, olive oil, olives
Smith Winery & Vineyard	Sierra Gold	10	Grapes (wine)
Somerset Gourmet	Sierra Gold	15	Fruit, grapes (wine), vegetables, nuts
Sonoma Mission Farms	North Coast	6	Grapes (Cabernet Sauvignon), olive oil, olives
Spottswoode Estate Vineyards	North Coast	43	Grapes (Cabernet Sauvignon), grapes (wine), olive oil, olives
SRJC Shone Farm Vineyard	North Coast	8	Grapes (Sauvignon Blanc)
Staglin Family Partners, Ltd	North Coast	42	Grapes (wine)
State Lane Vineyards	North Coast	13	Grapes (wine)

Producer	Chapter	Certified area (acres)	Certified products
Steve Ricetti Vineyards	Mendocino	3	Grapes (wine)
Stone Edge Vineyard	North Coast	10	Fruit, grapes (wine), vegetables, olive oil, olives
Storybook Mountain Vineyards	North Coast	43	Grapes (wine)
Sunstone Vineyards & Winery	South Coast	28	Grapes (wine)
Sunview Vineyards/ Sunview Marketing International	Kern	2181	Dehydration, uncultivated land, grapes, grapes (table), grapes (wine), persimmons, pomegranates, raisins
Terra D'Oro Vineyards	Sierra Gold	10	Grapes (wine)
Terra Linda Farms— Grape Division	Fresno-Tulare	251	Grapes, grapes (raisins), grapes (Syrah), grapes (wine
Lucas Cellar & Winery	Big Valley	3	Grapes (wine)
Napa Valley Reserve	North Coast	64	Grapes (wine), olives, trees
Poor Farm	Mendocino	82	Grapes, grapes (wine)
Thomas Hill Farm	San Luis Obispo	7	Grapes (wine), fruit and vegetables, persimmons
Thompson Vineyards	Mendocino	10	Grapes (Carignan), grapes (Petite Syrah)
Tomki Vineyards	Mendocino	41	Grapes (Cabernet Sauvignon), grapes (Merlot), wine
Top Of Konocti Farms	Mendocino	30	Grapes (wine), nuts
Topolos Vineyards, LLC	North Coast	50	Grapes (wine), grapes (Zinfandel)
Tres Sabores	North Coast	13	Grapes (wine), lemons, olives, pomegranates
Trimble Vineyards	Mendocino	11	Grapes (Cabernet Sauvignon), grapes (Carignan)
Turley Wine Cellars	North Coast	149	Grapes (Petite Syrah), grapes (wine), grapes (Zinfandel), olive oil, olives

Producer	Chapter	Certified area (acres)	Certified products
Turner Vineyard	South Coast	21	Grapes (Chardonnay), grapes (Pinot Noir), grapes (Syrah), grapes (wine)
Uhlich Vineyard	Big Valley	18	Grapes (Cabernet Sauvignon)
Ulysses Lolonis Vineyards	Mendocino	21	Grapes (Carignan), grapes (Petite Syrah), grapes (Zinfandel)
Uncle Bob Vineyards	Mendocino	2	Grapes (Cabernet Sauvignon), grapes (Pinot Noir)
Upton Vineyards	Mendocino	18	Grapes (Petite Syrah), grapes (Sangiovese), grapes (Sauvignon Blanc), nuts
Usibelli Farm & Game	North Coast	31	Grapes (Cabernet Sauvignon)
V. Sattui Winery	North Coast	29	Grapes, grapes (Cabernet Sauvignon), grapes (Mourvèdre), grapes (Petit Verdot), grapes (Syrah), grapes (Zinfandel)
Vau Investments	Mendocino	35	Grapes, grapes (Cabernet Sauvignon)
Vecino Vineyards	Mendocino	40	Grapes (Pinot Noir), grapes (Sauvignon Blanc), grapes (Syrah)
Viluko Farms	Central Coast	44	Almonds, apples, artichokes, asparagus, basil, beetroot, blueberries, carrots, chard, cherries, coriander, corn, cucumber, dill, eggplant, fennel, garlic, grapes, grapes (Cabernet Sauvignon), grapes (Chardonnay), grapes (Petit Verdot), grapes (Sauvignon Blanc), green cabbage, Japanese medlars, melons, nectarines, olives, onions, peaches, pears, peppers...

Producer	Chapter	Certified area (acres)	Certified products
Viluko Farms (continued)	Central Coast	44	... pistachios, plums, pomegranates, potatoes, pumpkins, raspberries, squashes tarragon, tomatoes, turnips, nuts
Vincent Brigantino Vineyards	Central Coast	5	Grapes (Cabernet Sauvignon)
Vittorio Vineyards	Mendocino	17	Grapes (wine)
Volker Eisele Vineyard	North Coast	57	Grapes (wine)
Wehr-Wagner Vineyards	North Coast	1	Grapes (wine)
Welch Vineyard Inc.—Management Department	Mendocino	65	Grapes, grapes (wine)
West Coast Vineyard, Inc.	Fresno-Tulare	120	Grapes (wine)
Western Botanical Medicine	Humboldt-Trinity	12	Uncultivated land, grapes (wine), plant extracts (dyes), grasses
Wild Hare Vineyard	Mendocino	6	Grapes (Merlot), nuts
Wild Hog Farm	North Coast	5	Grapes (wine)
Wilde Wolf Vineyards	North Coast	5	Grapes (Cabernet Sauvignon)
Wolford Vineyard	Mendocino	10	Grapes (wine)
Wulf Vineyards	Fresno-Tulare	29	Grapes (wine)
Y & V Organic Farm	Pacific Southwest	50	Avocados, fruit, grapefruit, grapes (wine), lemons, oranges
Yorkville Vineyards	Mendocino	33	Grapes (wine), wine
Yount Mill Vineyards	North Coast	608	Grapes (wine), olives
ZD Wines	North Coast	32	Grapes (wine), olives, wine

Appendix B
Labeling Rules
TTB 5190.11 for Organic Wine Labeling– Rev. 06/2009

Guidelines for Labeling Wine as "100% Organic"

This document contains a sample label. It should be used as guidance relating to the National Organic Program (NOP) regulations at 7 CFR (Code of Federal Regulations) part 205. To view these regulations in their entirety, please visit the United States Department of Agriculture's website at www.ams.usda.gov/ nop. This sample complies with the Federal Alcohol Administration Act, the Alcohol Beverage Labeling Act and the NOP.

When labeling your product as "100% Organic," it must contain 100 percent organically produced ingredients and have been processed using organically produced processing aids, not counting added water and salt. You should also consider the following points in designing your label:

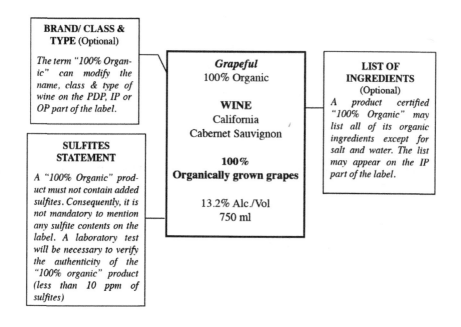

BRAND/ CLASS & TYPE (Optional)

The term "100% Organic" can modify the name, class & type of wine on the PDP, IP or OP part of the label.

SULFITES STATEMENT

A "100% Organic" product must not contain added sulfites. Consequently, it is not mandatory to mention any sulfite contents on the label. A laboratory test will be necessary to verify the authenticity of the "100% organic" product (less than 10 ppm of sulfites)

Grapeful
100% Organic

WINE
California
Cabernet Sauvignon

100%
Organically grown grapes

13.2% Alc./Vol
750 ml

LIST OF INGREDIENTS
(Optional)
A product certified "100% Organic" may list all of its organic ingredients except for salt and water. The list may appear on the IP part of the label.

DECLARATION OF
CERTIFICATE
(mandatory)
"Certified Organic by ..."
or similar expression must
appear under the name
and address of the bottler
for domestic wines, or of
the importer for interna-
tional wines. This certification may be posted on
the IP part of the label and
can include the name,
telephone number or web-
site of the Certification
Agency.

Grapeful
100% organic
Wine

PRODUCED & BOTTLED BY:
GRAPEFUL WINERY, SOLIS,
CALIFORNIA
CERTIFIED ORGANIC BY:
ABC organic certifiers

GOVERNMENT WARNING: (1)
ACCORDING TO THE SURGEON
GENERAL, WOMEN SHOULD NOT
DRINK ALCOHOLIC BEVERAGES
DURING PREGNANCY BECAUSE
OF THE RISK OF BIRTH DEFECTS.
(2) CONSUMPTION OF ALCOHOLIC
BEVERAGES IMPAIRS YOUR ABILI-
TY TO DRIVE A CAR OR OPERATE
MACHINERY, AND MAY CAUSE
HEALTH PROBLEMS.

USDA ORGANIC
SEAL
(Optional)
The USDA seal confirm-
ing a 100% Organic
Product may appear on
the PDP, IP or OP part of
the label.

SEAL OF THE
CERTIFICATION
AGENCY
(Optional)
The seal of the USDA
approved Agency for
Organic Certification
can be added to the label
of a 100% Organic Prod-
uct (PDP, IP or OP).

Key

PDP (Principle Display Panel)

The part of the label that is most likely to be displayed, presented, shown, or examined under customary conditions of display for sale.

IP (Information Panel)

The part of the label of a packaged product that is immediately contiguous to and to the right of the principal display panel as observed by an individual facing the principal display panel, unless another section of the label is designated as the information panel because of package size or other attributes (e.g., irregular shape with one usable surface).

OP (Other Panel)

Any panel other than the principal display panel, information panel, or ingredient statement.

IS (Ingredient Statement)

The list of ingredients contained in a product shown in their common and usual names in the descending order of predominance

DEPARTMENT OF AGRICULTURE
AGRICULTURAL MARKETING SERVICE
WASHINGTON, DC 20250, USA

DEPARTMENT OF THE TREASURY
ALCOHOL AND TOBACCO TAX AND TRADE BUREAU
WASHINGTON, DC 20220, USA

Publication of TTB 5190.11 for Oganic Wine Labeling

Guidelines for Labeling Wine as "Organic"

This document contains a sample label. It should be used as guidance relating to the National Organic Program (NOP) regulations at 7 CFR (Code of Federal Regulations) part 205. To view these regulations in their entirety, please visit the United States Department of Agriculture's website at www.ams.usda.gov/nop. This sample complies with the Federal Alcohol Administration Act, the Alcohol Beverage Labeling Act and the NOP.

When labeling your product as "Organic," it must contain at least 95 percent organically produced ingredients, not counting added water and salt. In addition, your product must not contain added sulfites and may contain up to 5 percent non-organically produced agricultural ingredients allowed by 7 CFR 205.606 (provided your accredited certifying agent has determined the ingredients to be not commercially available in organic form), and/or other substances allowed by 7 CFR 205.605. You should also consider the following points in designing your label:

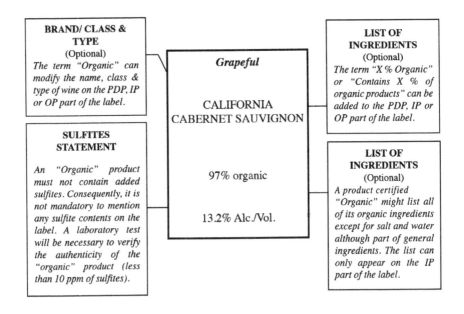

BRAND/ CLASS & TYPE
(Optional)
The term "Organic" can modify the name, class & type of wine on the PDP, IP or OP part of the label.

Grapeful

CALIFORNIA CABERNET SAUVIGNON

97% organic

13.2% Alc./Vol.

LIST OF INGREDIENTS
(Optional)
The term "X % Organic" or "Contains X % of organic products" can be added to the PDP, IP or OP part of the label.

SULFITES STATEMENT

An "Organic" product must not contain added sulfites. Consequently, it is not mandatory to mention any sulfite contents on the label. A laboratory test will be necessary to verify the authenticity of the "organic" product (less than 10 ppm of sulfites).

LIST OF INGREDIENTS
(Optional)
A product certified "Organic" might list all of its organic ingredients except for salt and water although part of general ingredients. The list can only appear on the IP part of the label.

Key
PDP (Principle Display Panel)

The part of the label that is most likely to be displayed, presented, shown, or examined under customary conditions of display for sale.

IP (Information Panel)

The part of the label of a packaged product that is immediately contiguous to and to the right of the principal display panel as observed by an individual facing the principal display panel, unless another section of the label is designated as the information panel because of package size or other attributes (e.g., irregular shape with one usable surface).

OP (Other Panel)

Any panel other than the principal display panel, information panel, or ingredient statement.

IS (Ingredient Statement)

The list of ingredients contained in a product shown in their common and usual names in the descending order of predominance.

DEPARTMENT OF AGRICULTURE
AGRICULTURAL MARKETING SERVICE
WASHINGTON, DC 20250, USA

DEPARTMENT OF THE TREASURY
ALCOHOL AND TOBACCO TAX AND TRADE BUREAU
WASHINGTON, DC 20220, USA

Publication of TTB 5190.11 for Organic Wine Labeling

Guidelines for Labeling Wine as "Made with Organic Ingredients"

This document contains a sample label. It should be used as guidance relating to the National Organic Program (NOP) regulations at 7 CFR (Code of Federal Regulations) part 205. To view these regulations in their entirety, please visit the United States Department of Agriculture's website at www.ams.usda.gov/ nop. This sample complies with the Federal Alcohol Administration Act, the Alcohol Beverage Labeling Act and the NOP.

When labeling your product as "Made with Organic Ingredients" (or a similar phrase), it must contain at least 70 percent organically produced ingredients, not counting added water and salt. In addition, wine may contain added sulfites (in accordance with 7 CFR 205.605) and may contain up to 30 percent non-organically produced agricultural ingredients and/or other substances allowed by 7 CFR 205.605. You should also consider the following points in designing your label:

DECLARATION OF CERTIFICATE (Optional) *The term "Made from Organic__ "[mentioning the Ingredient(s) or group of ingredients] may appear of the PDP, IP or OP part of the label.*	*Grapeful* CALIFORNIA CABERNET SAUVIGNON Made with organic grapes 13.2% Alc./Vol.

THE LABELS MUST NOT SHOW THE USDA ORGANIC SEAL

DECLARATION OF PERCENTAGE (Optional)	*Grapeful* **75% organic ingredients** **Wine**	USDA ORGANIC SEAL (Optional)

DECLARATION OF PERCENTAGE
(Optional)
The term "Made from X % of Organic Ingredients" or "X % Organic" or similar expression may appear on the PDP, IP or OP part of the label.

LIST OF INGREDIENTS
(Optional)
Products certified, "Made from organic ingredients" might list all their ingredients and use the term Organic to identify the concerned ingredients (to the exception of salt and water). They may appear as such only on the IP part of the label.

Grapeful
75% organic ingredients
Wine

Ingredients: Organic Cabernet Sauvignon Grapes, CONTAINS SULFITES

PRODUCED & BOTTLED BY:
GRAPEFUL WINERY, SOLIS, CALIFORNIA
CERTIFIED ORGANIC BY:
ABC organic certifiers

GOVERNMENT WARNING: (1) ACCORDING TO THE SURGEON GENERAL, WOMEN SHOULD NOT DRINK ALCOHOLIC BEVERAGES DURING PREGNANCY BECAUSE OF THE RISK OF BIRTH DEFECTS. (2) CONSUMPTION OF ALCOHOLIC BEVERAGES IMPAIRS YOUR ABILITY TO DRIVE A CAR OR OPERATE MACHINERY, AND MAY CAUSE HEALTH PROBLEMS.

USDA ORGANIC SEAL
(Optional)
The USDA seal may be used for an organic product and can appear on the PDP, IP or OP part of the label.

SEAL OF THE CERTIFICATION AGENCY
(Mandatory)
"Certified Organic by …" or similar expression must appear under the name and address of the bottler for domestic wines or of the importer for international wines. This certification may be posted on the IP part of the label and can include the name, telephone number or website of the Certification Agency.

Key
PDP (Principle Display Panel)

The part of the label that is most likely to be displayed, presented, shown, or examined under customary conditions of display for sale.

IP (Information Panel)

The part of the label of a packaged product that is immediately contiguous to and to the right of the principal display panel as observed by an individual facing the principal display panel, unless another section of the label is designated as the information panel because of package size or other attributes (e.g., irregular shape with one usable surface).

OP (Other Panel)

Any panel other than the principal display panel, information panel, or ingredient statement.

IS (Ingredient Statement)

The list of ingredients contained in a product shown in their common and usual names in the descending order of predominance.

DEPARTMENT OF AGRICULTURE
AGRICULTURAL MARKETING SERVICE
WASHINGTON, DC 20250, USA

DEPARTMENT OF THE TREASURY
ALCOHOL AND TOBACCO TAX AND TRADE BUREAU
WASHINGTON, DC 20220, USA

TTB 5190.11 for organic wine labeling

Guidelines for Labeling Wine as
"Made with Organic and Non-organic Ingredients"

This document contains a sample label. It should be used as guidance relating to the National Organic Program (NOP) regulations at 7 CFR (Code of Federal Regulations) part 205. To view these regulations in their entirety, please visit the United States Department of Agriculture's website at www.ams.usda.gov/nop. This sample complies with the Federal Alcohol Administration Act, the Alcohol Beverage Labeling Act and the NOP.

When labeling your product as "Made with Organic and Non-Organic Ingredients" (or a similar phrase), the label must indicate the presence of non-organic grapes in the "Made with Organic..." statement on the label, and such wine must contain at least 70 percent organically produced ingredients, not counting added water and salt. In addition, wine may contain added sulfites (in accordance with 7 CFR 205.605) and may contain up to 30 percent non-organically produced agricultural ingredients and/or other substances allowed by 7 CFR 205.605. You should also consider the following points in designing your label:

<table>
<tr>
<td>
DECLARATION OF CERTIFICATE
(Optional)

The term "Made from Organic__ [name of ingredient(s)] and non-organic__[name of ingredient(s)]" may appear of the PDP, IP or OP part of the label.
</td>
<td>
Grapeful

CALIFORNIA
CABERNET SAUVIGNON

Made with Organic Grapes
& Non-Organic Grapes
</td>
</tr>
</table>

THE LABELS MUST NOT SHOW THE USDA ORGANIC SEAL

DECLARATION OF PERCENTAGE (Optional)	*Grapeful* **75% organic ingredients** **Wine**	USDA ORGANIC SEAL (Optional)

DECLARATION OF PERCENTAGE
(Optional)
The term "Made from X % of Organic Ingredients" or "X % Organic" or similar expression may appear on the PDP, IP or OP part of the label.

LIST OF INGREDIENTS
(Optional)
Products certified "Made from organic ingredients" might list all of their ingredients. The word Organic can be used to identify specific ones (to the exception of salt and water although part of ingredients) and name them as such on the IP part of the label only.

Grapeful
75% organic ingredients
Wine

Ingredients: Organic Cabernet Sauvignon Grapes, Merlot grapes, CONTAINS SULFITES

PRODUCED & BOTTLED BY: GRAPEFUL WINERY, SOLIS, CALIFORNIA
CERTIFIED ORGANIC BY: ABC organic certifiers

GOVERNMENT WARNING: (1) ACCORDING TO THE SURGEON GENERAL, WOMEN SHOULD NOT DRINK ALCOHOLIC BEVERAGES DURING PREGNANCY BECAUSE OF THE RISK OF BIRTH DEFECTS. (2) CONSUMPTION OF ALCOHOLIC BEVERAGES IMPAIRS YOUR ABILITY TO DRIVE A CAR OR OPERATE MACHINERY, AND MAY CAUSE HEALTH PROBLEMS.

USDA ORGANIC SEAL
(Optional)
The USDA seal can be used on organic products and may appear on the PDP, IP or OP part of the label

DECLARATION OF CERTIFICATE
(mandatory)
"Certified Organic by ..." or similar expression must appear under the name and address of the bottler for domestic wines or of the importer for international wines. This certification may be posted on the IP part of the label and can include the name, telephone number or website of the Certification Agency.

Key
PDP (Principle Display Panel)
The part of the label that is most likely to be displayed, presented, shown, or examined under customary conditions of display for sale.

IP (Information Panel)
The part of the label of a packaged product that is immediately contiguous to and to the right of the principal display panel as observed by an individual facing the principal display panel, unless another section of the label is designated as the information panel because of package size or other attributes (e.g., irregular shape with one usable surface).

OP (Other Panel)
Any panel other than the principal display panel, information panel, or ingredient statement.

IS (Ingredient Statement)

The list of ingredients contained in a product shown in their common and usual names in the descending order of predominance.

DEPARTMENT OF AGRICULTURE
AGRICULTURAL MARKETING SERVICE
WASHINGTON, DC 20250, USA

DEPARTMENT OF THE TREASURY
ALCOHOL AND TOBACCO TAX AND TRADE BUREAU
WASHINGTON, DC 20220, USA

TTB 5190.11 for organic wine labeling

Guidelines for Labeling Wine Restricted to an "Organic Ingredients" Statement

This document contains a sample label. It should be used as guidance relating to the National Organic Program (NOP) regulations at 7 CFR (Code of Federal Regulations) part 205. To view these regulations in their entirety, please visit the United States Department of Agriculture's website at www.ams.usda.gov/nop. This sample complies with the Federal Alcohol Administration Act, the Alcohol Beverage Labeling Act and the NOP.

This sample label is applicable to the production of wines by wineries exercising an exemption from certification found at 7 CFR part 205.101(a)(3) or 7 CFR part 205.101 (a)(4). Products exempt from certification may contain less than 70 percent organically produced ingredients, not counting added water and salt. In addition, the product may contain over 30 percent non-organically produced agricultural ingredients and/or other substances without being limited to those in 7 CFR 205.605. The term "organic" shall only appear in an ingredient statement and the accompanying percentage statement. You should also consider the following points in designing your label:

<table>
<tr><td align="center">Grapeful

CALIFORNIA RED WINE

13.2% Alc./Vol.

750 ml</td></tr>
</table>

THE LABELS MUST NOT SHOW:
The USDA Organic Seal
The Certifying Agent Seal
A Certification Statement
The Term "Organic" in the Absence of an Ingredient Statement

<table>
<tr>
<td>

DECLARATION OF PERCENTAGE
(product containing organic and non-organic ingredients)
(Mandatory)
The term "Made from X % of Organic Ingredients" or "X % Organic" or similar expression must appear on the IP part of the label.

</td>
<td>

Grapeful

Ingredients: Organic Cabernet Sauvignon Grapes, Merlot grapes, tartaric acid, CONTAINS SULFITES

75% organic ingredients

PRODUCED & BOTTLED BY: GRAPEFUL WINERY, SOLIS, CALIFORNIA

GOVERNMENT WARNING: (1) ACCORDING TO THE SURGEON GENERAL, WOMEN SHOULD NOT DRINK ALCOHOLIC BEVERAGES DURING PREGNANCY BECAUSE OF THE RISK OF BIRTH DEFECTS. (2) CONSUMPTION OF ALCOHOLIC BEVERAGES IMPAIRS YOUR ABILITY TO DRIVE A CAR OR OPERATE MACHINERY, AND MAY CAUSE HEALTH PROBLEMS.

</td>
<td>

LIST OF INGREDIENTS
(Optional)
Products limited to the declaration "Made from Organic Ingredients" may list all of their organic ingredients. The term "organic" can only be used to identify specific ingredients and their percentage. Water and Salt, although part of the ingredients, will not be listed as "organic ingredients". This list cannot appear on the IP.

</td>
</tr>
</table>

DECLARATION OF PERCENTAGE
(product containing organic ingredients only)
(Mandatory)
If a wine presents a list of "Organic" ingredients but do not list any "Non-organic" ingredients it must then be made from 100% of organic ingredients. The label must not show any percentage.

Key

PDP (Principle Display Panel)

The part of the label that is most likely to be displayed, presented, shown, or examined under customary conditions of display for sale.

IP (Information Panel)

The part of the label of a packaged product that is immediately contiguous to and to the right of the principal display panel as observed by an individual facing the principal display panel, unless another section of the label is designated as the information panel because of package size or other attributes (e.g., irregular shape with one usable surface).

OP (Other Panel)

Any panel other than the principal display panel, information panel, or ingredient statement.

IS (Ingredient Statement)

The list of ingredients contained in a product shown in their common and usual names in the descending order of predominance.

DEPARTMENT OF AGRICULTURE
AGRICULTURAL MARKETING SERVICE
WASHINGTON, DC 20250, USA

DEPARTMENT OF THE TREASURY
ALCOHOL AND TOBACCO TAX AND TRADE BUREAU
WASHINGTON, DC 20220, USA

Appendix C
Main Events in the Wine Industry and Professional Trade Fairs

Main Events in the Wine Industry
March

World Competition for Riesling, Gewürztraminer, Pinot Gris and Sylvaner + Trade fair for white grape varieties

12th Annual Opolo dinner for Zinfandel vintners

Barbecue weekend at the Zinfandel Festival

Buy and sell a winery or a vineyard

Introduction to tasting room management

The paradise of Pinot

WiVi Central Coast

ProWein

Japan: International Food and Beverage Exhibition (FOODEX)

California: Natural Products Expo West

Belgium: Expo4Bio

April

UC Davis University professional wine program

INTERVITIS INTERFRUCTA

China International Organic Food Industry Expo

United Kingdom: Natural and Organic Products Europe

May

WSWA convention and exhibition

London International Wine Fair

Next Organic Berlin

BioFact China

Korea: 14th Environment-Friendly Organic Framing Trade Show

June

Vineyard business seminar

Northwest Wine Expo | Texas

Direct

Vinexpo

Netherlands: Sustainable Foods Summit Europe

BioFact America Latina, Brazil

July

ASEV National Conference

Annual Conference for the Eastern ASEV

Wine industry technology symposium

WineTech

Organic viticulture conference

International Pinot Noir Festival

August

Wine bloggers conference

September

Annual Conference of the Oenology Professors Society

November

Annual Symposium on wine industry financing

Wine Tourism Conference

Professional Trade Fairs
January

Unified symposium on wine and the vine—Sacramento, California

February

Annual assembly of the association of wine grape producers of Washington—Kennewick, Washington

March

Zinfandel Weekend in Paso Robles—Paso Robles, California

Licenses in the three-level system and your winery—Rohnert Park, California

Organic—from the grape to the glass—Rohnert Park, California

Annual Opolo dinner for Zinfandel vintners—Paso Robles, California

Barbecue weekend at the Zinfandel Festival—Paso Robles, California

Annual summit of Pinot Noir—San Francisco, California

Creating value in the wine industry—Rohnert Park, California

WiVi Central Coast—Paso Robles, California

The Paradise of Pinot—Campbell, California

An Introduction to tasting room management—Rohnert Park, California

Buying and selling a winery or a vineyard—Rohnert Park, California

Descriptive analysis of white and red table wines—Davis, California

Pre-sale celebration of the Mackinaw Trail winery—Petoskey, Michigan

ProWein—Düsseldorf, Germany

UC Davis University professional wine program–Davis, California

Communicating about sustainability–San Francisco, California

Independent vintners propose a marketing seminar about wine grapes–Paso Robles, California

April

Presentation on allergens in wine–St. Helena, California

Annual unified symposium on vines and wine–Dobson, North Carolina

Concrete strategies for increasing online wine sales–Rohnert Park, California

Social media and wine marketing–Rohnert Park, California

The World Competition for Riesling, Gewürztraminer–Strasbourg, France

Innovative marketing of wine and brand dynamics–Rohnert Park, California

Good practices for wineries using QuickBook–Rohnert Park, California

UNLVino–Bubble-Licious–Las Vegas, Nevada

Annual practical training on membranes and filtration/separation technologies–College Station, Texas

Management accounting for your wine business–Rohnert Park, California

Budgets, forecasts and good practices for your wine business–Rohnert Park, California

UNLVino, Sake Fever–Las Vegas, Nevada

Winemakers festival–Solvang, California

UNLVino, Grand Tasting–Las Vegas, Nevada

UNLVino, BAR-b-q–Las Vegas, Nevada

EnVision ReVision–Rohnert Park, California

INTERVITIS INTERFRUCTA–Stuttgart, Germany

The DNA of consumer satisfaction–Rohnert Park, California

Today's channels for selling wines–Rohnert Park, California

May

WSWA convention and exhibition–Orlando, Florida

Annual Cinco de Mayo Golf Classic–Napa, California

"Pack your bags"–For vintners' kids–Healdsburg, California

Vintners dinner at the Wine Festival–Paso Robles, California

ZinFest: Wine, food and entertainment at Lake Lodi–Lodi, California

Hood River Rotary presents the 3rd Annual Columbia Gorge Wine & Pear Fest–Hood River, Oregon

London International Wine Fair–London, UK

Vine legends dinner–Madera, California

June

Vineyard business seminar–Napa, California

A celebration of wine–Madera, California

Napa Valley Auction–Napa, California

Northwest Wine Expo | Texas–Dallas, Texas

Wine bloggers conference Penticton–British Columbia, Canada

Barbera Festival–Plymouth, California

ZD Winery & head chef of Sensi, Roy Ellamar–Las Vegas, Nevada

Direct–Napa, California

Vinexpo–Bordeaux, France

July

ASEV National Conference–Monterey, California

Blending festival–Paso Robles, California

WineTech–Sydney, Australia

Wine industry technology symposiu–Napa, California

Annual Conference for the Eastern ASEV–Winston-Salem, North Carolina

"The importance of soil and geology in the taste of the terroir, a case study of the Willamette Valley"–Various venues, Oregon

Annual Catalan Festival–Sonoma, California

Gold medal wine tasting–Seattle, Washington

Organic winemaking conference–St. Helena, California

August

International Pinot Noir Festival–McMinnville, Oregon

Annual Conference of the Oenology Professors Society–Orlando, Florida

International Indiana Wine Competition–West Lafayette, Indiana

Annual Symposium on wine industry financing–Napa, California

Wine Tourism Conference–Portland, Oregon

APPENDIX D
The Price of Some Organic Wines in the United States

Region	Color	Appellation	Name	Vintage	AB	CL	RP in USD
Napa Valley	Red	Cabernet Sauvignon	Joseph Phelps	2012	Organic	75	59.99
Napa Valley	Red	Cabernet Sauvignon	Round Pond Estate Rutherford	2012	Organic	75	57.99
North Coast California	Red	Cabernet Sauvignon	Bonterra	2012	Organic	75	14.99
Oregon	Red	Pinot Noir	Willamette Valley Vineyards Estate	2012	Organic	75	29.99
Napa Valley	Red	Cabernet Sauvignon	Frog's Leap Estate	2012	Organic	75	49.99
Central Coast California	Red	Pinot Noir	Ventana Arroyo Winery	2012	Organic	75	17.99
California	Red	Zinfandel	Michael David Winery	2012	Organic	75	17.99
Napa Valley	White	Sauvignon Blanc	Frog's Leap	2014	Organic	75	15.99
Central Coast California	White	Chardonnay	Hess Select	2013	Organic	75	13.99
North Coast California	Red	Pinot Noir	Deovlet La Encantada	2012	Organic	75	49.99
Napa Valley	White	Chardonnay	Grgich Hills	2011	Organic	75	39.99
California	Sparkling	White	Korbel	NV	Organic	75	14.99
Oregon	Sparkling	Rosé	Argyle Brut	NV	Organic	75	49.99
Sonoma County	White	Gewürztraminer	Alexander Valley Vineyards	2013	Organic	75	10.99
Columbia Valley	White	Riesling	Pacific Rim	2012	Organic	75	15.99
Sierra Foothills, California	White	Riesling	Domaine Cazes	2008	Organic	37.5	8.9

Source: www.wines.com, April 2015

APPENDIX E
Californian Organic Wines

Some Recommendations
Hall Wines, Cabernet Sauvignon 2010 (Organic)

HALL believes that the health of the environment is essential. They will make every effort in their vineyard management to ensure the health of our ecosystems. HALL St. Helena Winery incorporates all structural requirements to qualify for the U.S. Green Building Council's Leadership in Energy and Environmental Design (LEED®) Green Building Rating System.

Domaine Carneros, Pinot Noir 2008 (Made from Organic Grapes)

"Winemaking begins with impeccable fruit, most of it grown in the certified organic estate vineyards. There is no formula. You have to be attuned to the rhythm of the grapes, the pulse of the wine." says Founding Winemaker Eileen Crane. In 2007, all of the estate vineyards received organic certification from the California Certified Organic Farmers (CCOF).

The Vegan, Vine Red Wines (Made from Organic Grapes)

Vegan Vine Wines are produced by Clos LaChance Wines in sunny San Martin.

In early 2009, Clos LaChance's 150-acre Estate vineyard was one of seventeen California vineyards to be Sustainably Certified via the California Sustainable Winegrowing Alliance.

Badger Mountain N.S.A. Organic Cabernet Sauvignon 2007 (Organic Winemaking & Viticulture)

Using a palette of diverse organic grapes, winemaker Jose Mendoza creates a wide array of classic varietal wines with no sulfites added. Jose's imaginative blends result in fresh and provocative wines " each with a distinct heady balance of fruit, floral, spice, and earth. Each of our NSA wines carries the USDA Organic logo and, per federal regulations, contains less than 10 parts per million sulfites."

Coturri P. Coturri Family Vineyard Zinfandel 2003 (Organic Winemaking & Viticulture)

Like all of the vineyards grown and maintained by the Coturris, no pesticides, fungicides, or herbicides are ever used on the Estate vineyard, and it is certified by the CCOF. In 1996, Tony and Phil Coturri earned top honors from the Sonoma Valley Ecology Center for Environmentally Friendly Business Practices with their viticultural farming and winemaking practices.

Bonterra Mendocino County Zinfandel 2006 (Organic Viticulture)

There's certified organic and then there's the spirit of organic—their grapes are 100% of both. "Each and every vine has its own mood, and our viticulturists know them all. Biodynamic® practices don't replace organic growing, they complement it." Today, Bonterra is considered by most as the leading California wine made with organic grapes and Bob Blue is one of the most recognized winemaker in the organic community.

Ceago Vinegarden "Del Lago" Chardonnay 2007 (Organic Viticulture)

In 1993, Jim Fetzer established Ceago Vinegarden. Jim concentrates on sound farming practices using biodynamic and organic methods to produce quality grapes. Farming using Biodynamic® practices requires a new way of understanding nature in which we perceive the living, form-giving forces that actively regulate the growing process of the plants, animals and soils. A certified Biodynamic® farm meets all the USDA and California standards for organic agriculture, as well as those specific to Biodynamic® farming.

Montinore Estate Willamette Valley, Gewürztraminer 2006 (Biodynamic Viticulture)

Established in 1982, Montinore Estate is a 210-acre Demeter Certified Biodynamic® and Stellar Certified Organic estate that lies at the northern end of the Willamette Valley appellation and along the east-facing slope of the Coastal Range foothills in Oregon.

Sky Saddle Chardonnay 2006 (Biodynamic Viticulture)

Committed to local sustainable agriculture, Sky Saddle is a small family wine business in Sonoma County making fine wines exclusively from organic and/or biodynamic grapes. The 2007 Zinfandel won a Double Gold Medal in the Organic & Biodynamic Wine Competition and a Gold Medal in the NextGen Wine Competition. The 2006 Chardonnay also won a Silver Medal in the NextGen Competition.

Cooper Mountain, Pinot Noir Mountain Terroir 2006 (Biodynamic Viticulture)

In 1987, the winery opened to offer its first vintage to the public. By 1995 CMV obtained organic certification from Oregon Tilth. Today all of Cooper Mountain's wines are certified organically grown. They now farm more than 100 acres, grow five varietals and are committed to sustainability: organic and biodynamic farming and winemaking as well as dry farming.

Mendocino Farms 2004 Redvine Series (Biodynamic)

They are a biodynamic winery, which means they are making wine as naturally as possible. Instead of using science to create the plumpest grapes imaginable, they use natural grapes to get a pure taste. Mendocino Farms gets the grapes for their wines from three vineyards. They are: Heart Arrow, Fairbairn, and Dark Horse Ranches. All three of these vineyards are biodynamic as certified by Demeter.

Bibliography

General Bibliography

Delmas, and L. Grant. *"Eco-labeling strategies: the eco-premium puzzle in the wine industry."* AAWE, Working Paper 13, 2008

Dion R. *Histoire de la vigne et du vin en France, des origines au XIXe siècle.* Paris, Flammarion, 768 p., 1959

Elias N. *La Civilisation des mœurs,* 1939, French transl. 1973, republished. Pocket, 2003

Enjalbert H. *Histoire de la vigne et du vin, l'avènement de la qualité.* Paris, Bordas, 208 p., 1975

Flandrin J.L. and Montanari M. *Histoire de l'alimentation.* Fayard, 1996

Joly N. *Le vin, du ciel à la terre : la viticulture en biodynamie.* Sang De La Terre, 229 p., 2003

Joly N. *Le vin, la vigne et la biodynamie.* Sang De La Terre, 304 p., 2007

Karlsson, B. & P. *Biodynamic, organic and natural wine making.* Floris Books, 260 p., 2012

Lichine A. *Encyclopédie des vins et des alcools de tous les pays.* Bouquins, 850 p., 1998

Pitte J.-R. *Gastronomie française. Histoire et géographie d'une passion.* Paris, Fayard, 266 p., 1991

Pivot B. *Dictionnaire amoureux du vin.* Plon, 2006

Rowley A., Ribault J.-C. *Le vin: une histoire de goût.* Gallimard, 159 p., 2003

Schirmer R. *Des Vignobles et des vins à travers le monde.* A tribute to A. Huetz de Lemps, symposium held in Bordeaux October 1–3, 1992,

Le Gars C., Roudié P., (dir.), Talence, Bordeaux University Press, coll. *"Grappes et millésimes,"* coll. *"Maison des pays ibériques."* n° 66, CERVIN, 656 p., 1996

Schirmer R. *La viticulture bio, une nouvelle modernité.* French-Québecois symposium: "Quality Products for Quality landscapes." Die, France 2004

Schirmer, R. *Une nouvelle planète des vins.* Conference at the International Geography Festival, Saint-Dié (September 30–October, 3 2004), "Feed men, feed the world," Geographers sit down to eat. Read more at: http://fig-st-die.education.fr

Atlas

Raphaël Schrimer, Hélène Vélasco-Graciet. *Atlas mondial des vins, la fin d'un ordre consacré ?* Paris, Autrement, 2010.

Hugh Johnson, Jancis Robinson. *Atlas mondial du vin.* Paris, Flammarion, 352 p., 2001

Pascal Ribereau-Gayon (Dir.). *Atlas Hachette des vins de France.* Hachette, INAO, 300 p., 2000

Articles from the Press

"*Le vin Bio est-il vraiment dégueu?*" Revue Terra Eco, July 2013
http://www.terraeco.net/vin-bio-vin-naturel-bon-gout-prix,49562.html

"*Tout savoir sur le vin bio*" La revue du vin de France
http://www.larvf.com/,vins-bio-agriculture-biologique-vins-naturels-
environnement-pesticides,10339,4023890.asp

"*Vins biologiques : l'alliance du goût et de l'environnement*" Huffington Post, Fabrizio Bucella, June
2012
http://www.huffingtonpost.fr/fabrizio-bucella/vins-biologiques-alliance-gout-
environnement_b_1617376.html

"*Du vin bio, du vin bon ?*" Revue Sens
http://www.sens.fr/tradi/sensorielle/du-vin-bio-du-vin-bon/

"*Faîtes votre marché: les succès des vins bio*" Le Figaro Vin, 13/11/2012
http://avis-vin.lefigaro.fr/connaitre-deguster/o34364-faites-votre-
marche-le-succes-des-vins-bios

Filmography

Wine from here, Martin Carel and Matthieu Tangay-Carel with natural wine producers in
California, 2011
http://winefromhere.com/

Les terroiristes du Languedoc, Ken Payton, 2012

La clef des terroirs, Guillaume Bodin, 2011
http://www.laclefdesterroirs.com/

Mondovino, Jonathan Nossiter, 2004

The Wine Business Library

ORGANIC WINE: A MARKETER'S GUIDE
Béatrice Cointreau

Building on detailed case studies, Cointreau presents an exhaustive analysis of global production and market trends, and provides clear insights on how to position one's product to the best effect.

$29.95
ISBN 978-1935879633
Pub Date: October 1, 2015
Paperback, 6 x 9 inches,
200 pp., graphs and charts

HOW TO IMPORT WINE: AN INSIDER'S GUIDE
Debra M. Gray

$29.95
ISBN 978-1-934259-61-0
Paperback, 7 x 9 inches,
288 pp., 200 illustrations,
charts, and fully indexed

THE EXPORTER'S HANDBOOK TO THE US WINE MARKET
Debra M. Gray

$29.95
ISBN 978-1-935879-51-0
Paperback, 7 x 9 inches,
210 pp., 100 illustrations,
charts, and fully indexed

WINE BUSINESS CASE STUDIES: THIRTEEN CASES FROM THE REAL WORLD OF WINE BUSINESS MANAGEMENT
Pierre Mora, Editor

Published in association with the Bordeaux College of Business, this book applies business pedagogy's powerful learning tool to the unique challenges of wine business management. *Wine Business Case Studies* is written by an international group of respected wine business scholars.

$30.00
ISBN 978-1-935879-71-8
Paperback, 8.5 x 11 inches,
300 pp., graphs and charts

THE BUSINESS OF WINEMAKING
Jeffrey L. Lamy

Places all facets of the wine business in perspective for investors, owners, and anyone else who is interested in how the wine business operates.

$45.00
ISBN 978-1-935879-65-7
Paperback, 7 x 10 inches,
360 pp., 250 illustrations,
charts, graphs, and fully indexed

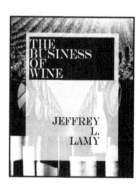

WINE MARKETING ONLINE
Brue McGechan

The whole wired realm of wine marketing is revealed in this encyclopedic yet readable and easy-to-follow guide.

$29.95
ISBN 978-1-935879-87-9
Paperback, 6 x 9 inches,
418 pp., illustrations and fully indexed

HOW TO LAUNCH YOUR WINE CAREER
Liz Thach, Ph.D. & Brian D'Emilio, foreword by Michael Mondavi

Career coaching from two of wine's most respected professionals and scores of industry icons like winemaker Heidi Barrett and writer James Laube of the *Wine Spectator*.

$29.95
ISBN 978-1-934259-06-1
Paperback, 6 x 9 inches,
354 pp., fully indexed

The Viticulture and Enology Library

CONCEPTS IN WINE TECHNOLOGY, SMALL WINERY OPERATIONS
Yair Margalit, Ph.D.

Revised and updated, this detailed how-to guide, written by physical chemist and winemaker Yair Margalit, is organized in the sequence of winemaking, and is both an excellent text for the classroom and a concise guide for the practicing winemaker.

$40.00
ISBN 978-1-935879-80-0
Hardcover, 7 x 10 inches,
320 pp., illustrations, charts,
graphs, and fully indexed

WINE FAULTS: CAUSES, EFFECTS, CURES
John Hudelson, Ph.D., foreword by John Buechsenstein

A precise and comprehensive description of the problems encountered at times by all winemakers and wine judges. Every microbial infection found in today's wineries is fully described and arrayed in full-color slides.

$39.95
ISBN 978-1-934259-63-4
Paperback, 8.5 x 11 inches,
96 pp., full-color illustrations
and fully indexed

CONCEPTS IN WINE CHEMISTRY, 3RD EDITION
Yair Margalit, Ph.D.

In this new edition of his classic text, Yair Margalit gives complete and current pictures of the basic and advanced science behind the biochemistry of vilification, making the updated *Concepts in Wine Chemistry* the broadest and most meticulous book on the topic in print.

$89.95
ISBN 978-1-935879-81-7
Hardcover, 7 x 10 inches,
550 pp., illustrations, charts,
graphs, and fully indexed

BIODYNAMIC WINE, DEMYSTIFIED
Nicholas Joly, foreword by Mike Benziger & Joshua Greene

Joly shares the core philosophy behind biodynamic viticulture and explains why the use of foreign substances disrupt vineyard ecology and are ultimately counterproductive to a wine's best, consistent expression.

$24.95
ISBN 978-1-934259-02-3
Paperback, 6 x 9 inches,
180 pp., color plates and
fully indexed

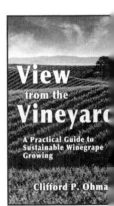

UNDERSTANDING WINE TECHNOLOGY, 3RD EDITION
David Bird, foreword by Hugh Johnson

This completely revised and updated edition deciphers all the new scientific advances that have cropped up in the last several years and conveys them in Bird's typically clear and plainspoken style.

$44.95
ISBN 978-1-934259-60-3
Paperback, 6 x 8 inches,
328 pp., full-color
illustrations, charts, and
fully indexed

VIEW FROM THE VINEYARD: A PRACTICAL GUIDE TO SUSTAINABLE WINEGRAPE GROWING
Clifford P. Ohmart, Ph.D.

This comprehensive examination of the subject provides the farmer with a path to a sustainable vineyard and concludes with a self-assessment guide in which growers can easily track their progress.

$34.95
ISBN 978-1935879909
Hardcover, 7 x 10 inches,
240 pp., color and fully
indexed